Thrive

Guide to

Flourishing in Retirement

Six Pathways to a Joyful Next Chapter

Beth Eifert

Thrive Guide to Flourishing in Retirement
by Beth Eifert

ISBN: 979-8-9945305-1-1

Table of Contents

For every brave soul stepping into the unknown with open hands, open eyes, and an open heart.

This guide is for you.

Introduction

Welcome to Your Thrive Guide

"The trouble with retirement is that you never get a day off."
- Abe Lemons

Let's face it: retirement is complicated. We spend years dreaming about it—slow mornings, finally learning to play the guitar, maybe even a little spontaneous travel (or at least spontaneous napping). And yes, there's a lot of freedom to celebrate. But once the novelty fades, it's not uncommon to feel...well, a little unmoored.

You're no longer tethered to a 9-to-5, but you might also feel like you've wandered off the map. The days are suddenly wide open, but the rhythm that used to anchor you has disappeared. Retirement doesn't just give you more time—it hands you a new identity and says, "Good luck with that!"

That's where this guide comes in.

Beyond the Numbers: What Makes a Life

Most retirement books are obsessed with your bank account—like money is the only thing standing between you and a good life. Please. A full wallet doesn't tell you how to fill your days, or what makes you laugh until your sides hurt.

Thriving in retirement is less about spreadsheets and more about what gets you out of bed in the morning (even if it's just for more coffee). It's about what grounds you, what delights you, and what reminds you that you're still very much you—even without the business cards.

That's why this guide is built around the Thrive Compass—your map for the road ahead, with six essential pathways to help you thrive:

"You can't change the wind, but you can adjust your sails."
- Aristotle

Spiritual Meaning: Chasing what gives you purpose, whether it's volunteering or finally understanding your cat's existential crisis.
Mental Clarity: Keeping your brain sharp, because forgetting where you parked is one thing, but losing your spark is another.
Social Connection: Finding your people, the ones who make you laugh or listen when you ramble.
Emotional Balance: Feeling all the feels without letting those feelings redecorate your entire house.
Physical Vitality: Having the energy to chase grandkids or at least the ice cream truck.
Financial Confidence: Trusting you've got enough to live the life you want, without panic-Googling "budget spreadsheets" at 2 a.m.

These areas don't exist in isolation – strengthening one often uplifts another. The goal here is to help you notice where you're thriving, where you're stretching, and where a small shift could make a big difference.

Spoiler Alert: You're Going to Want a Journal

Reflection works best when you can capture it. Whether you're a write-in-the-margins type or a digital minimalist, have something nearby to jot in. A journal, a Google Doc, a napkin pile—just make it yours.

You'll be surprised how much insight you already have once you start paying attention.

How it Works

This guide won't ask you to read it from start to finish (who has the time?). It's designed more like a field companion—something structured enough to orient you, but flexible enough to let you wander where you need to.

Think of it like a Fodor's guide for the soul. No hotel ratings, but plenty of internal landmarks.

In Chapter 1, you'll begin with two reflective exercises: first curating your most meaningful life moments, then envisioning a day in your ideal retired life. These aren't just warm-ups; they create a foundation—a personal blueprint you'll carry forward. By clarifying what matters most, you'll have a lens to interpret everything that follows.

In Chapter 2, you'll take the Thrive Assessment: part reflection, part reality check, and arguably the heart of this whole guide. Think of it as your first compass reading. With your reflections in mind, you'll see how the six pathways of thriving are showing up in your life right now. This snapshot helps you spot imbalances, uncover quiet strengths, and identify where a little extra attention could go a long way.

From there, you'll jump to the chapter that feels most relevant in this moment. Each chapter helps you quickly hone where to focus by showing you what "great" can look like in that area, and how to move in that direction with targeted, doable exercises.

Think of it as practical wisdom, not generic advice. You'll also find Pocket Notes: short prompts to help you jot, doodle, or muse your way toward a little more clarity. This isn't about filling out every page or getting gold stars. Note what sparks something. Skip what doesn't. You're not being graded—you're mapping.

Over time, your Thrive Journal will become less of a workbook and more of a personal atlas—something that shows where you've been, what's working, and what you want more of. Because thriving isn't a one-time achievement—it's a practice. And this guide will be here whenever you need a little recalibration, a little courage, or just a place to think things through with a pen in your hand and your feet on the floor.

My Own Journey: Two Very Different Paths

"The afternoon knows what the morning never suspected."
- Robert Frost

Before we dive into the rest of the guide, I'd like to share how I got here—because like many of you, I wasn't entirely sure what to expect when the rhythms of working life fell away.

I found retirement to be one big, messy life shift—equal

parts exciting and disorienting. It was like setting out on a hike with a backpack full of granola bars and no map. The landscape was wide open and strangely unfamiliar. And here's the thing: everyone navigates it differently.

Take my husband, Jim, for example.

After 41 years in the military, I assumed he'd need at least a year to decompress. Read some books. Stare at the water. Watch golf with the volume up. But the moment he retired, it was like he'd been waiting all his life for this next chapter. Think of the movie, Yes Man, meeting civic engagement:

Coach a U-9 soccer team? Yes, please.

Join Rotary? Absolutely.

Become a guardian ad litem for foster kids? Sign me up!

Within weeks, his calendar was fuller than it had been while working. He jumped in with both feet.

I, on the other hand, am more of a "dip one toe in and see if the water's warm" kind of person. Instead of filling my days, I studied retirement itself. I earned a retirement transition coaching certification to better understand this stage—not just for myself, but for anyone else tiptoeing into this terrain.

Looking back, I now see how we were each drawing from different parts of the Thrive Compass. Jim found purpose and connection through service, drawing on the social dimension. I leaned into reflection and recalibration, focusing on mental clarity and emotional balance.

To this day he's still saying yes to everything with enthusiasm, and I'm still making space to figure out what's next. Neither approach is right or wrong—they're just different chapters of the same story.

And that's the point: there's no one way to thrive. Some people need structure and a full calendar. Others need stillness, space, and maybe a really good pen. This guide is here to meet you wherever you are—whether you're racing into a new life, like Jim, or wandering toward it more slowly, like me. In the chapters ahead, you'll reflect on your story, sketch your vision, and check your compass—so you can step forward with confidence.

Thriving, Your Way

"Tell me, what is it you plan to do with your one wild and precious life."
- Mary Oliver

Retirement isn't about what you're leaving behind. It's about what you're stepping into. It's reinvention, reflection, and yes—a few wrong turns along the way.

This guide isn't chasing perfection. It's about showing up for yourself with curiosity, resilience, and a bit of humor—even on the days when thriving feels like a stretch.

So, grab a coffee, a pen, and a quiet corner. Let's begin your next chapter—imperfect, beautiful, and entirely yours. Welcome to your thriving life.

Chapter One

Discovering Your Thriving Life

Retirement advice is often full of "shoulds"—you should travel more, volunteer, downsize, move somewhere warm, take up pickleball. (Not that I'm anti-pickleball. Unless it's before coffee.) But what if instead of racing ahead to a prefab vision of what life should look like, you paused to ask a different question: What has always made you feel most like yourself?

This chapter invites you to slow down and explore that question through two lenses: reflection and imagination. First, you'll walk through a discovery exercise to surface the moments when you've felt most alive, most grounded, most aligned. It's not about nostalgia. It's about pattern recognition. These moments are breadcrumbs, and they often point toward the kind of life your future self will thrive in.

Then, you'll use that clarity in a visioning exercise to imagine your ideal day in retirement. The order matters. Too often, people jump to dreaming without asking if their dreams actually match who they are. By beginning with lived experience, you create a foundation that makes your vision both meaningful and actionable.

Together, these two exercises form your launch pad for the Thrive Assessment in Chapter 2. They give you real-life evidence and a future picture, so when you assess the six pathways of thriving, you'll know what you're aiming for and why it matters.

Exercise 1: The Life That's Most You

"You are what you repeatedly do. Excellence, then, is not an act, but a habit."
- attributed to Aristotle

What This Is About

We spend a lot of time trying to figure out what we should be doing with our lives, usually by watching what everyone else is doing. Volunteering. Starting foundations. Launching goat-yoga retreats in Bali.

But your purpose isn't in someone else's highlight reel. It's in your own behavior—what you do when you feel most alive.

In this exercise, you'll collect real-life moments from your own story, the times when you felt most like yourself. These moments aren't random memories; they're clues. By curating them, you'll begin to see patterns emerge.

Whether you complete this in a single sitting or stretch it out over weeks, the effort is worth it. After all, it took a lifetime to accumulate them, any reflection is a step toward clarity.

Let's find the through-line in your life that's already there. No reinvention necessary. And as you gather these moments, remember this isn't the whole picture. In the next exercise, you'll use the clarity you uncover here to imagine a future day in retirement that reflects those same patterns.

1. Gather Your Moments (20-30 minutes)

In your journal, list 10–20+ moments from your life when you felt most like yourself. Write a 1–3 sentence description for each. Include childhood, early adulthood, family life, solo experiences, and recent days. Think of this as curating the highlight reel of your most authentic moments. Label your collection: *Moments I Felt Most Like Myself.*

2. Reflect on the Patterns (20-30 minutes)

Look across your entries and ask:

- What emotions consistently show up?
- Are you mostly solo, with a partner, in a group?
- What kinds of places appear repeatedly?

Circle keywords, underline repeated themes, or use color-coding to tag patterns. Don't overthink—just look for the threads that connect your most meaningful experiences.

3. Spot the Soul of Your Style (10 minutes)

Ask:

- What personal strengths repeat?
- Where do I feel grounded, curious, or fulfilled?
- What settings or roles keep surfacing?

You don't need to label it neatly. Simply notice the shape of your "life style" as it reveals itself in motion.

4. Check Your Alignment (10 minutes)

Alignment simply means that your choices, rhythms, and priorities match the life that feels most like you. Maybe this exercise confirms you've already been living that way – or maybe it highlights a few places that feel slightly off course. Either way, you're holding a kind of map now, a record of your truest style of living.

Ask yourself:

- *Am I still curious?*
- *Am I still stretching into the outer edges of my style?*
- *Are my choices—big and small—aligned with my compass?*

This isn't about setting goals. It's about remembering what's already true—and deciding if you want to live even more deeply from that place.

Exercise 2: Your Ideal Retired Life

Now that you've uncovered the patterns in your own story, it's time to look forward. In this exercise, you'll carry those insights into a vision of your ideal retired life.

What This Is About

Planning or reimagining your retired life is a bit like hosting the perfect dinner party: it sounds delightful, but once you start thinking about the details—who's coming, what's on the menu, where to seat Uncle Bob—you realize it takes a little effort to get it right. The good news? You're the host and the guest of honor, so you get to call all the shots.

"Imagination is everything. It is the preview of life's coming attractions."
- Albert Einstein

Studies show that visualization isn't just wishful thinking, it's a powerful tool for shaping decisions and behaviors *(Pham & Taylor, 2024)*. By mentally rehearsing your ideal outcomes, you create a roadmap that aligns your daily choices with your bigger vision.

So, let's set the scene: imagine a day in the life of your best retired self. As you walk through the prompts, jot your responses in your notebook or journal. Let it be fluid and honest. There's no "correct" version—only yours.

A Day in the Life Prompts

- *You're waking up. What time is it, and what's the first thing you do? Are you savoring coffee in bed, meditating, or heading out for a brisk walk? How does it feel to start the day your way?*
- *Look around. Where are you, and who's sharing this moment with you? Is it a partner, a friend, a pet, or maybe just the sunshine streaming through your favorite window?*
- *Breakfast time! What's on your plate? What does this meal say about how you care for yourself?*
- *The day begins to unfold. What are you excited about today? Is it something creative, productive, or purely for fun?*
- *Mid-morning rolls around. What keeps your mind sharp and engaged? Are you diving into a book, starting a blog, or otherwise challenging yourself?*
- *It's lunchtime. Where are you, who's with you, and what makes this meal memorable?*
- *The afternoon is yours. Are you creating, exploring, learning, or simply savoring the peace? How do you strike the balance between being active and letting yourself relax?*
- *Who do you connect with during the day? How do these relationships make you feel, and how do you nurture them?*
- *Dinner time arrives. Who's at the table with you, and what's the conversation about? What brings you joy in these moments?*
- *As the evening winds down, what's your favorite way to reflect on the day? Do you journal, meditate, or share your thoughts with someone special?*
- *Finally, as you prepare for tomorrow, what gives you a sense of calm and fulfillment? How do you feel as you drift off to sleep?*

Bringing It All Together

Now step back and look at what you've gathered—both your curated moments and your envisioned day. These are not just memories or fantasies; they're your personal blueprint, woven from real experience and honest aspiration.

Together, these two exercises give you both a rear view mirror and a windshield. One shows you the essence of who you've always been. The other shows you what kind of future would honor that essence. With both in hand, you're ready for the Thrive Assessment—the next step in spotting where your life today aligns with your vision, and where you might want to shift the balance.

If you have a spouse or partner, consider asking them to do these exercises as well. You're not aiming for identical visions - most couples can't even agree on dinner - but sharing what you each discovered often leads to honest, energizing conversations. It's a simple way to understand each other's hopes a little better and to make sure you're walking into this next chapter with fewer surprises and more "Oh, that actually makes sense."

Trail Marker: Your most authentic life is already speaking through the moments you've lived and the visions you hold. The more you listen, the clearer the map becomes

Chapter Two

Assessing Your Thrive Compass

You've done the inner work in Chapter 1: curating your most authentic moments and envisioning a day in your thriving retired life. With that clarity in hand, it's time for a gentle reality check: your first compass reading. The Thrive Assessment offers you a snapshot of how those visions line up with your life today, pointing you toward the areas that may be asking for a little more attention.

This is not a test, but a gentle orientation. A way of asking: Where am I standing now, in relation to the life I long to live?

Think of it like checking the map before a road trip: you're not lost, you're just seeing where you stand before deciding where to go next. Let's dive in.

How It Works

If you've still got that coffee, great. If not, no worries—this is just you and the page now. On the next spread, you'll find 30 statements grouped under the six pathways of thriving. For each, circle the number that best matches how true it feels for you today:

- 5 = Very true
- 4 = Mostly true
- 3 = Somewhat true
- 2 = Rarely true
- 1 = Not true at all

Go with your gut, no overthinking (we've all got enough of that). The whole thing should take about 5–10 minutes.

Remember: your answers are a snapshot, not a verdict. Think of this as a bridge between vision and action. Your scores will help you decide which part of the Thrive Compass to explore first, guiding you toward the remedies most likely to spark energy and ease.

The Thrive Assessment

SPIRITUAL MEANING

I feel a deep sense of connection to something larger than myself.

1 2 3 4 5

My actions align with my personal values.

1 2 3 4 5

I have a strong sense of purpose in my life.

1 2 3 4 5

I make time to feel grateful, even for the small stuff.

1 2 3 4 5

I consistently engage in my spiritual practices.

1 2 3 4 5

MENTAL CLARITY

I can focus on tasks without my mind wandering.

1 2 3 4 5

I make decisions in a timely manner.

1 2 3 4 5

I tackle problems by following a clear, orderly method.

1 2 3 4 5

I actively seek opportunities to learn new things.

1 2 3 4 5

I know what's most important in my life right now.

1 2 3 4 5

SOCIAL CONNECTION

I'm genuinely curious about what others have to say.

1 2 3 4 5

I lend a hand when someone needs it.

1 2 3 4 5

I stay connected to different social groups.

1 2 3 4 5

I set boundaries kindly while respecting those of others.

1 2 3 4 5

I nurture close ties with family and friends.

1 2 3 4 5

EMOTIONAL BALANCE

I handle stress without losing my cool (most of the time).

1 2 3 4 5

I'm okay sharing my feelings with those I trust.

1 2 3 4 5

I bounce back quickly from setbacks or disappointments.

1 2 3 4 5

I can let go of grudges and forgive others.

1 2 3 4 5

I process my emotions in a way that feels healthy.

1 2 3 4 5

PHYSICAL VITALITY

I move my body regularly throughout the day.

1 2 3 4 5

I eat wholesome foods often.

1 2 3 4 5

I get 7-9 hours of restful sleep most nights.

1 2 3 4 5

I stay on top of checkups and preventive care.

1 2 3 4 5

I steer clear of overdoing things like alcohol or caffeine.

1 2 3 4 5

FINANCIAL CONFIDENCE

I spend within my means, no panic required.

1 2 3 4 5

I've got an emergency fund for life's surprises.

1 2 3 4 5

I regularly check my investments to make sure they still meet my goals.

1 2 3 4 5

I have the insurance I need, just in case.

1 2 3 4 5

I feel good about where my finances stand.

1 2 3 4 5

Reviewing Your Results

Now comes the fun part: seeing what your answers reveal about your life right now. No pressure, no judgment—just information you can use.

Add up your scores for each dimension (Spiritual, Mental, Social, Emotional, Physical, Financial), then divide each total by 5 to get an average for that area.

Your averages give you a snapshot of where you're steady and where you may want to lean in a little more. Here's a simple way to read them:

- **4–5** → You're in a strong spot here.
- **3 or below** → You may want to focus here.

Remember, no score is "bad." Life shifts, seasons change, and your needs evolve. These numbers simply shine a light on where you might invest a little extra attention right now.

Pocket Reflection

"Awareness is the first step in change."
- Nathaniel Branden

Pause with your journal and consider:

- *How do these results connect or clash with the blueprint you sketched in Chapter 1?*
- *Which area surprised you with its strength?*
- *Which felt a little neglected or tender?*
- *Did any themes or patterns emerge?*
- *Where do you feel naturally drawn to begin?*

Jot down a few words, a phrase, or a sentence. Don't overthink it, just capture what's rising to the surface.

Moving Forward

With this assessment complete, you now have a clearer picture of where you're feeling steady and where you're being invited to grow.

Some readers begin with the pathway that scored lowest; others choose the one that feels most important right now. There's no wrong path. Each chapter stands on its own, but together they form a toolkit for building the thriving life you envisioned in Chapter 1.

Keep in mind: thriving isn't about fixing yourself. It's about returning to what's already good and true and expanding from there, one conscious choice at a time. You're already on your way. Let's keep going.

Trail Marker: Your scores aren't destinations—they're signposts. Each one points to a place where small attention can spark big shifts toward thriving.

Chapter Three

Spiritual Meaning – The Inner Spark to Wholeness

If your Thrive Compass guided you here, you might be feeling a quiet ache for meaning—or maybe just a vague sense that something feels a little...off. Like your inner compass is spinning but not quite pointing north. The beliefs or routines that once grounded you might feel worn thin, or maybe life's transitions have stirred up old questions you thought were already boxed and labeled.

Whatever brought you here, this chapter isn't about having tidy answers. It's about getting curious—about what lights you up, what centers you, and what makes you feel like you again. It's spiritual well-being without the incense (unless you're into that).

The Quick Start below will guide you gently as you reflect, realign, and reconnect to what feels most true—not in some grand, mountaintop way, but in small, meaningful ways that matter in the real world.

QUICK START

How to Use This Chapter

📖 **Step 1: Start with "Mapping the Terrain."**
Get a feel for why spiritual meaning matters and how it weaves into your thriving life.

👁 **Step 2: Explore "What Great Looks Like."**
Scan the statements in this section. Note when something resonates or sparks recognition.

🔔 **Step 3: Reflect on "Warning Signs."**
Move to the "Warning Signs" section. Scan and note any that feel familiar, even if it's just a small tug of recognition.

🔍 **Step 4: Pinpoint "Possible Causes."**
In this section, gently explore the list. Linger on any that resonate with your current spiritual experience, like a puz-

zle piece clicking.

⚒ Step 5: Try "Remedies."

Use the Possible Causes you reflected on as a guide. Turn to the corresponding Remedy to find practical, actionable steps you can take.

Throughout, use the Pocket Notes prompts at the end of the chapter to reflect, capture insights, and shape any small next steps that feel meaningful to you.

🕮 Mapping the Terrain

Spiritual well-being is that part of you that craves more than to-do lists and the occasional "why am I here?" moment over coffee. It's about finding purpose, connecting to something bigger—whether that's faith, nature, or just the quiet hum of your own heart. Retirement's the perfect time to explore this, with no meetings or commutes to distract you.

What gives your days meaning? What do you believe when you've got a moment to think? This chapter invites you to wander through those questions—maybe with prayer, meditation, gardening, or just sitting still, no Wi-Fi required. You might reconnect with old values, let go of grudges, or lean into kindness and empathy, which have a sneaky way of bringing peace. Curiosity and openness can turn retirement into a season of growth, fulfillment, and maybe a little calm. Because who doesn't want that?

This exploration doesn't just lift your spirit—it ripples out, deepening your emotions, relationships, and even how you see time or money. "My Own Journey" below shares how spirituality can ebb and flow, not as a strict path but as a companion for your own unfolding. Then we'll dive into reflecting on your values, trying practices that feed your soul, and rediscovering what feels sacred now.

My own journey:

For me, spiritual well-being wasn't something I lost all at once—it slipped away quietly, like a boat drifting from shore. I grew up with Catholicism woven into the fabric of my life, and for years, I loved the structure of it. I loved the predictability, the rituals, the sense that someone, somewhere, had already worked out all the answers so I didn't have to. But then life happened, and I found myself stepping away. Not because I was angry, not because I didn't believe anymore, but because I wanted to see what else was out there.

What I found was both exhilarating and slightly unhinged. I tried all the things people tell you will bring a deep sense of inner peace. I journaled. I practiced mindfulness. I took long walks at sunset and tried to feel one with the universe—though mostly I just ended up swatting mosquitoes and thinking about what to make for dinner. And along the way, I realized something: spirituality wasn't about following a prescribed set of rules, nor was it about abandoning everything I had known. It was about finding presence. It was about noticing things—small things, beautiful things, fleeting moments that remind you that life is bigger than to-do lists and Costco runs.

I started seeing glimpses of the sacred in the most ordinary places. In the way my husband reaches for my hand when we cross the street. In a really good cup of coffee. In a stranger holding the door open without expecting a thank-you (though I always say thank you). And—this part surprised me—I started missing the very structure I had left behind. Not in the "I need to repent immediately" kind of way, but in the "maybe there was something to this all along" kind of way.

So I did what any reasonable person would do: I slowly found my way back, this time on my own terms. I realized that faith and personal spirituality didn't have to be opposing forces. That rituals can be both grounding and freeing. That belief can be less about certainty and more about showing up—even when you're not entirely sure what you're showing up for.

And that's the thing about spiritual well-being—it's not about having all the answers. It's about making space for the questions. Whether you find peace in prayer, poetry, gardening, or standing at the ocean's edge wondering if any of this makes sense, the important thing is that it means something to you. So, let's begin—not with rigid rules, but with curiosity. If we're lucky, this phase of life isn't just about coasting—it's about rediscovering what fills us up, and maybe, just maybe, finding a little peace along the way.

👁 What Great Looks Like

Here's what spiritual well-being feels like when it's humming along. These qualities show what's possible—not to chase perfection, but to spot what's already strong or where a small nudge could bring more spark. Scan and note any that resonate.

- Feels a keen sense of purpose.
- Regularly pauses to appreciate beauty and awe.
- Expresses gratitude daily.
- Nurtures resilience, discipline, and a forgiving heart.
- Feels joy and contentment in daily life.
- Embraces a balanced approach to 'being' and 'doing.'
- Maintains fulfilling connections and a sense of community.
- Accepts uncertainty with grace.

Notice where purpose, joy, or connection already lights up your days—and imagine how a small pause could make them shine brighter.

🔔 Warning Signs

These are gentle whispers that your spiritual side might need a little TLC, like a plant drooping for water. They're not about guilt—just a nudge to listen with curiosity. Take note of any that feel true for you.

- Feels lost or unsure of identity.
- Behavior does not align with values or beliefs.
- Lacks purpose or direction.
- Has difficulty finding beauty or joy in life's moments.
- Rarely experiences or expresses gratitude.
- Holds onto resentment or struggles to forgive.
- Seldom feels content with daily life.
- Feels driven to "do" rather than "be."
- Withdraws from social circle; feels isolated.
- Struggles to accept uncertainty or lack of control.

These signs are just your heart whispering for a little care—time to listen and reconnect.

🔍 Possible Causes

Sometimes spiritual drift happens so quietly that you don't notice how much disconnection, longing, or restlessness has taken root. These gentle signs can softly shape how you find meaning and peace in your days. The table below helps you name the drift. It pairs the most common underlying Causes with the Remedies that can help you feel oriented and alive again.

Review the list and note any Cause that speaks to you; then, jump to that Remedy in the next section. Or if you'd like more context, the explanations below the table describe each Cause more fully and can help you choose the remedy that best fits where you are.

Causes	Remedies
Lack of purpose	1. Reignite
Big life shifts or loss	2. Ground Yourself
Questioning old beliefs	3. Clarifying Values
Carrying old grudges	4. Practicing Forgiveness
Lost your sense of wonder	5. Developing Curiosity
Feeling disconnected	6. Building Connections
Rushing through life	7. Practicing Presence
Resisting change	8. Embracing Acceptance
Lost the spark of awe	9. Cultivating Awe
Fear of mortality	10. A Final Gift
Gratitude's gone quiet	11. Practicing Gratitude
Loss of identity	12. Reclaiming Self

Causes with Explanations

Lack of purpose or spiritual connection

If your days feel hollow or strangely disconnected, it could be a sign that your deeper compass has gone quiet. Without a sense of meaning, even ordinary routines can feel heavy or flat.

➔**See Remedy 1: Reignite** — *Clarify What Gives You Purpose* for simple ways to nurture direction and vitality.

Big life shifts or loss

Losing someone, retiring, or going through a major shift can uproot the familiar rhythms that once steadied you. Even joyful transitions can leave your spirit searching for new footing.

➔**See Remedy 2: Ground Yourself** — *Create One Meaningful Daily Ritual* to rebuild steadiness from within.

Questioning old beliefs

Beliefs that once felt sure now seem murky or in need of reexamination. When your internal framework starts shifting, it can create a lingering sense of spiritual unease.

➔**See Remedy 3: Clarifying Values** — *Your Compass for a Meaningful Life* to reconnect with what truly matters now.

Carrying old grudges

When old wounds or grudges stay tucked away, they quietly weigh down your emotional and spiritual vitality. Without space for forgiveness, resentment grows where peace could live.

➔**See Remedy 4: Practicing Forgiveness** — *Freeing Yourself From the Weight of the Past* to lighten your path.

Lost your sense of wonder

If the world feels unusually gray, repetitive, or uninspiring, your inner sense of wonder might be calling for attention. Curiosity often rekindles the spark that reconnects you to awe and meaning.

➔**See Remedy 5: Developing Curiosity** — *Embracing the Spirit of Wonder* to reawaken your sense of discovery.

Feeling disconnected from others

When conversations stay surface-level and emotional closeness feels rare, even familiar relationships can start to feel distant. Isolation may not happen all at once, but it qui-

etly erodes the spirit over time.
➔**See Remedy 6: Building Connections** — *Finding the Sacred in Relationships* to renew bonds that nourish you.

Rushing through life

You find yourself rushing through days, half-aware, checking off tasks without feeling truly immersed in your life. Without presence, even beautiful moments pass by unnoticed.
➔**See Remedy 7: Practicing Presence** — *Rediscover the Joy of Being Here* to reawaken your sense of wonder in the now.

Resisting change

When change feels like a personal threat instead of a natural part of life, tension builds. Resistance becomes a heavy load, making peace and flexibility harder to find.
➔**See Remedy 8: Embracing Acceptance** — *Finding Peace in Letting Go* to soften and adapt with grace.

Lost the spark of awe

If the world feels flat, predictable, or stripped of its magic, your sense of awe might be fading. Without those moments of marvel, even retirement's freedom can feel routine.
➔**See Remedy 9: Cultivating Awe** — *Open to the Wonder Around You* to rediscover the joy of pausing and marveling.

Fear of mortality or impermanence

Avoiding thoughts of death is human—but over time, that quiet fear can pull us away from peace, purpose, and those we love. We may delay making end-of-life plans, not out of indifference, but discomfort. Yet facing these choices, even gently, can be a powerful way to ease your own spirit and offer clarity to those you'll one day leave behind.
➔**See Remedy 10: A Final Gift** — *Peace for You, Clarity for Them* to turn avoidance into love-in-action.

Gratitude's gone quiet

If small joys no longer stir much feeling—or if gratitude feels mechanical rather than alive—your spirit may be

thirsting for deeper connection. Without active appreciation, even a beautiful life can feel distant.
➔**See Remedy 11: Practicing Gratitude** — *Cultivating Joy Through Noticing* to reconnect with appreciation.

Loss of Identity

When a role you once held dear—parent, partner, professional, provider—fades or changes, it can leave a quiet vacancy inside. You may still be busy, even grateful, but feel strangely undefined. That subtle sense of "Who am I now?" can erode spiritual grounding over time, making life feel less meaningful, even when things seem fine on the surface.
➔**See Remedy 12: Reclaiming Self** — *Remember Who You Are Beneath the Roles* to gently rediscover your inner foundation.

Remedies

⚒ This is your toolbox of practical, heartfelt steps to reconnect with purpose, wonder, and peace. Pick remedies based on the causes that resonate, or dip into any that spark curiosity. Use your journal to capture insights.

1
Reignite

Clarify What Gives You Purpose

A sense of purpose rarely arrives in a flash—it builds quietly through the moments that make you feel most alive. Maybe it's the spark you feel when helping others, or the energy that comes from creating something new. As you begin to notice the pattern, your life starts pointing in a clearer, more meaningful direction.

Why This Matters

When life starts to feel hollow or disoriented, it's often your inner compass calling for realignment. Research shows that a strong sense of purpose can increase life satisfaction by up to 20% *(Journal of Positive Psychology, 2020)*. Whether through a quiet habit or bold new pursuit, reconnecting with what lights you up can bring clarity, energy, and direction back into your days.

> *"The meaning of life is to find your gift. The purpose of life is to give it away."*
> *—Pablo Picasso*

☛ Try This: Craft Your Purpose Snapshot

Earlier in this guide, you explored the moments when you felt most like yourself—and envisioned a day that reflected your truest rhythms and values. Now, let's build upon that inner terrain with even sharper focus.

Pause and Reflect (5 min.)

In your journal, write down 3 moments in the last month or two when you felt truly you. Maybe it was a walk with a friend or fixing a recipe gone wrong. What made those moments feel alive? Were you creating, connecting, or simply present?

Identify Your Spark (3 min.)

From those moments, pick one word that captures what energized you (e.g., creativity, kindness, curiosity). *Example: If cooking felt joyful, your spark might be "nurturing."*

Take One Step (2 min.)

Choose a small action to honor that spark. If your word is "nurturing," cook a meal for a neighbor or plant a seed. Ask yourself: *What's one tiny way I can bring this spark into my day? How might this spark shape your days if you let it grow?*

Reflect & Write

- What fear might be nudging you away from bringing this spark into your day?

Quick Tip

Spend five minutes today noticing what brings you joy—it's a clue to your spark.

For Further Exploration

Book: *Man's Search for Meaning* by Viktor E. Frankl – A timeless guide to finding purpose in any season.

Podcast: *The Happiness Lab*, episode on "Purpose vs. Happiness" – Dr. Laurie Santos explores why meaning matters.

Try It: Spend 10 minutes this week exploring a hobby you loved as a kid. What feels familiar?

Trail Marker: A life of purpose is woven from the quiet threads you choose to notice.

---

2 Ground Yourself

Create One Meaningful Daily Ritual

Some actions are more than habits—they're small ceremonies that shape the way your day feels. Lighting a candle, walking the same quiet path, or saying a few words of thanks can become steadying rhythms when life feels loose around the edges. A single ritual, done with care, turns the ordinary into something quietly grounding.

Why This Matters

After a life transition, it's easy to feel a bit untethered. A daily ritual offers something to return to—a moment that's just yours, steady and quiet. These acts don't just organize your day; they sanctify it and can increase emotional resilience by up to 15% *(Mindfulness Journal, 2021).*

"Rituals are the formula by which harmony is restored."
—Terry Tempest Williams

☛ **Try This: Anchor Your Day**

Ready to anchor your day? This simple practice invites you to weave intention into a familiar moment—let's get started with a few easy steps.

Notice a Moment (2 min.)

Identify a part of your day that feels rushed or automatic—like brushing your teeth or making coffee.

Choose a Ritual (3 min.)

Add one intentional action to that moment: three deep breaths, one line of gratitude, lighting a candle. Keep it simple.

Try It Today (2 min.)

Practice your ritual once today. Pause and notice what shifts. How does this small pause feel?

Quick Tip

Stick with the same ritual for three days to build momentum.

Reflect & Write

- If this ritual were a symbol, what might it represent now?
- What quiet need did this moment seem to point toward?

For Further Exploration
Book: *The Miracle of Mindfulness* by Thich Nhat Hanh – A gentle and practical guide to reclaiming presence in small, everyday moments.
Podcast: *On Being* with Krista Tippett – Look for episodes featuring guests like Mary Oliver or Pico Iyer on sacred routines and stillness.
Try It: Choose a 2-minute ritual and practice it for three consecutive days. Record what you noticed after each practice in a notebook or your phone.

Trail Marker: A small act, repeated with care, becomes a sacred rhythm.

3 Clarifying Values

Your Compass for a Meaningful Life

As old rhythms fade, life can feel as if someone shuffled the map. Values are the landmarks that don't move. They shape how you show up, what you stand for, and where your energy naturally flows.

Why This Matters

Naming your values helps you live with greater clarity and peace. It's not about perfection—it's about alignment. When you live by your values, your time, choices, and relationships reflect who you really are. Studies show that living in alignment with your values can increase life satisfaction by over 20% *(Journal of Adult Development, 2020).*

☛ Try This: Discover Your Core Five

We don't often take time to name the values we hold most dear. This gentle exercise helps you uncover and live them. Let's begin with a few thoughtful steps.

Scan & Select (3 min.)

Read the list below and circle words that resonate with you.

"Values are like fingerprints. Nobody's are the same, but you leave them all over everything you do."
—Elvis Presley

Achievement	Collaboration	Faith	Learning
Adventure	Community	Family	Love
Affluence	Competence	Gratitude	Loyalty
Appreciation	Courage	Health	Recognition
Autonomy	Creativity	Humor	Self-respect
Balance	Duty	Harmony	Social ties
Challenge	Economic	Integrity	Spirituality
Change	Environment	Justice	Wisdom

Find Your Five (3 min.)

Narrow it down to the five that feel most essential to you in this season of life. Which values feel most alive in you right now?

Align & Act (3 min.)

For each of your top five, write one tiny action that would express that value today. Examples:
Creativity: Sketch for 10 minutes
Gratitude: Text someone a thank-you note
Health: Take a 15-minute walk

Quick Tip

Write your five values on a sticky note and place it where you'll see it daily—your fridge, desk, or bathroom mirror.

Reflect & Write

- Which values have I neglected lately?
- Where in my day do my values already shine through?

For Further Exploration

Book: *The Values Factor* by Dr. John Demartini – A practical framework for identifying and prioritizing what truly matters.

Podcast: *Life Kit* by NPR – Search for episodes on decision-making, authenticity, and living in alignment.

Try It: Pick one of your top five values and live it out intentionally for 7 days. Jot down one observation each day about how it shaped your mindset, choices, or energy.

Trail Marker: Your values are already in you—this just helps you hear them more clearly.

---

4 Practicing Forgiveness

Freeing Yourself from the Past

Some feelings overstay their welcome. Resentment may feel justified, even protective—but over time, it begins to weigh you down. Releasing what no longer serves you loosens the grip and makes space for peace again.

Why This Matters

Forgiveness isn't for them—it's for you. Letting go of resentment reduces stress, lightens emotional load, and restores inner peace. Research shows that practicing forgiveness can reduce depression and anxiety by over 25% *(Journal of Behavioral Medicine, 2019).* It's not about excusing the past—it's about freeing yourself to move forward.

"To forgive is to set a prisoner free and discover that the prisoner was you."
—Lewis B. Smedes

☛ Try This: Loosen the Grip

Let's ease into forgiveness together. This gentle practice guides you toward release—take these steps at your own pace.

Name the Weight (3 min.)

Identify a resentment or past hurt you're holding. Write a word or phrase that captures the essence of what still lingers.

Write & Reframe (3 min.)

Write a short letter expressing your pain—what hurt, what felt unfair. Then imagine their point of view. What might they have misunderstood, feared, or needed?

Choose a Release Ritual (3 min.)

Tear up the letter, burn it safely, or store it as a symbol of release. Then write:
"I am ready to let go of this pain and reclaim my peace."

Quick Tip

Forgiveness is a process. Repeat this exercise anytime

old pain resurfaces.

Reflect & Write

- What pain am I still holding that no longer serves me?
- How might forgiveness free up energy for joy or purpose?

For Further Exploration
Book: *The Book of Forgiving* by Desmond and Mpho Tutu – A roadmap to healing emotional wounds through forgiveness.
Podcast: *Ten Percent Happier* – Look for episodes on resentment, compassion, and letting go.
Try It: Write a forgiveness intention and tape it somewhere private. Read it aloud for seven days. Pay attention to any internal shifts.

Trail Marker: Forgiveness isn't weakness—it's the courage to stop carrying what hurts.

5 Developing Curiosity

Embracing the Spirit of Wonder

Curiosity might just be the secret ingredient to a vibrant spiritual life. It's a subtle invitation to explore, turning the familiar into a canvas for wonder and growth. Even the smallest question—Why this? What if?—can stir something luminous beneath the surface of an ordinary day.

Why This Matters

In retirement, routines can dull the spirit. Curiosity rekindles wonder and reveals new paths. As author and Modern Elder Chip Conley put it, "A routine is a habit without a soul." Left unchecked, even our most cherished rituals can become hollow. Cultivating curiosity brings movement to your inner life and creates space for awe.

☛ Try This: Follow a Thread of Curiosity

Take a moment to awaken your curiosity. This gentle practice invites you to explore new paths—proceed with

> "I have no special talent. I am only passionately curious."
> —Albert Einstein

these steps at your leisure.

Pick Your Spark (2 min.)

Choose a spiritual idea, text, or practice that tugs at your attention—something unfamiliar, intriguing, or long postponed. It might be:

- A book or sacred text
- A meditation or breathing technique
- A philosophical or spiritual question
- A tradition from another culture

Engage Slowly (3 min.)

Spend a few minutes with it today. Read a passage, try a short exercise, or reflect on one small idea. Let it breathe. Let it surprise you.

Reflect Without Judgment (2 min.)

Pause and ask: What stirred in me? What questions remain? Note any thoughts or emotions that surface—no matter how incomplete.

Quick Tip

Curiosity isn't about mastering something. It's about showing up to meet it.

Reflect & Write

- What new questions or practices are quietly tugging at me?
- Where have I assumed something "wasn't for me" before truly exploring it?

For Further Exploration

Book: *The Untethered Soul* by Michael A. Singer – A graceful dive into curiosity as a gateway to freedom and spiritual openness.

Podcast: *The Next Big Idea* – Look for episodes on awe, creativity, or personal reinvention.

Try It: Spend 10 minutes this week with a spiritual idea you've nearly explored. You don't need to master it—just meet it.

Trail Marker: Curiosity doesn't require answers — just the courage to ask and listen.

6 Building Connections

Finding the Sacred in Relationships

Spirituality often shows up in human form—in shared laughter, deep listening, or the warmth of simply being seen. These sacred ties can anchor you when old roles slip away.

Why This Matters

Relationships are where we practice grace and love in real time. One meaningful conversation can re-root you in what matters. Studies show strong social bonds can boost purpose and health by 20% *(American Psychological Association, 2022)*, while loneliness is more harmful to health than smoking 15 cigarettes a day *(Holt-Lunstad, 2010, PLoS Medicine)*.

"Connection is why we're here; it is what gives purpose and meaning to our lives."
—Brené Brown

☛ **Try This: Rebuild or Rekindle**

Step into the joy of connection. This practice offers a pathway to rebuild relationships—move forward with these gentle steps.

Pause and Recall (3 min.)

In your journal, name one person or group that once brought you joy. What made that connection special?

Take a Small Step (4 min.)

Send a thoughtful message, invite them for coffee, or explore a new way to connect (e.g., a class or volunteer project). *Example: A quick "Thinking of you" text to an old friend.*

Notice the Shift (2 min.)

After connecting, pause and feel the moment. Did it lighten your day or spark new thoughts?

Quick Tip

Try one reconnection a week to build your circle.

Reflect & Write

- What might hold me back from more?

- How might a new bond enrich my days?

For Further Exploration
Book: *The Gifts of Imperfection* by Brené Brown – A guide to authentic connections.
Podcast: *The Happiness Lab* by Dr. Laurie Santos – Episodes on belonging.
Try It: Send a "thinking of you" note this week and note what unfolds.

Trail Marker: One connection can root you—reach out and grow.

7 Practicing Presence

Rediscover the Joy of Being Here

Presence transforms the everyday into holy ground: the quiet magic of sunlight on water or the lift of a friend's laughter. These are quiet invitations to savor life's sacred ordinary.

Why This Matters

Retirement may offer more time, but presence is what gives that time depth. It reconnects you to joy, gratitude, and wonder—the parts of life that can so easily fade into the background. Studies show that even brief daily acts of awareness and awe can measurably boost emotional resilience and happiness *(UCSF Big Joy Project, 2023).*

☛ Try This: Create a Sacred Pause

Embrace the moment with care. This practice guides you to create a sacred pause—follow these steps with intention.

Choose a Break (3 min.)

Pick a daily moment (e.g., after coffee, before sunset, etc) to pause. When do I feel ready to slow down?

Breathe and Notice (4 min.)

When that moment arrives, take three slow breaths. Notice the space around you: the light, the air, the sounds, life moving quietly.

"Be—don't try to become."
—Osho

Thank Yourself (2 min.)
Silently thank yourself for simply being present. How does this feel without doing?

Quick Tip

Practice your pause daily—it deepens with time.

Reflect & Write

- What typically distracts me from being present?
- How can I invite more "being" and less "doing" into my daily rhythm?

For Further Exploration
Book: *The Power of Now* by Eckhart Tolle – A guide to living in the moment.
Podcast: *On Being* with Krista Tippett – Episodes on wonder and being.
Try It: Start each day with a 1-minute pause before tasks.

Trail Marker: Presence is a gift—unwrap it in every breath.

8 Embracing Acceptance

Finding Peace in Letting Go

Life unfolds with its own rhythm, and acceptance weaves peace into that dance. Letting go isn't giving up—it's softening your grip on what you can't control. That gentle release clears space for calm to return.

Why This Matters

We often cling to control, but loosening that grip opens space for joy. As the well-known Stoic, Marcus Aurelius, wrote, "Receive without pride, let go without attachment." Letting go is how we return to center—lighter, freer, and more at peace with what is.

☛ **Try This: Loosen Your Grip**
Journey toward peace with ease. This practice offers

steps to loosen your hold—move through them at your own rhythm.

Spot the Tension (3 min.)

Notice one moment today where you feel tense or controlling. Was it planning dinner? Worrying about someone's choices? Wanting an event to unfold perfectly? Ask yourself: What happens if I loosen my grip just a little?

Pause and Breathe (4 min.)

Take three slow breaths and ask, "What if I let go a little?"

Take a Small Step (2 min.)

Allow someone else to pick the restaurant. Stay silent instead of offering advice. Allow a plan to unfold without adjusting it.

"The greatest gift you can give yourself is a little bit of your own attention."
—Anthony J. D'Angelo

Reflect & Write

- What shifted when I let go? What fear might linger?
- What would trusting the flow of life feel like – even just for today?

Quick Tip

Practice one let-go moment daily to build peace.

For Further Exploration

Book: *The Tao of Pooh* by Benjamin Hoff – A gentle guide to flowing with life.

Podcast: *On Being* with Krista Tippett – Episodes on acceptance and surrender.

Try It: Let one decision unfold naturally today and reflect.

Trail Marker: Peace grows where you let go—trust the dance.

9 Cultivating Awe

Open to the Wonder Around You

Awe sneaks into life through a starry sky or a child's giggle, inviting you to pause and marvel. It's a subtle gift that turns the ordinary into magic.

Why This Matters

Retirement opens space for wonder, yet daily routines can dim that spark, leaving life feeling flat or predictable. As philosopher Abraham Heschel noted, "Wonder is the sense of the mystery of being," a quiet force that reconnects you to the world's beauty, offering resilience against life's monotony and a deeper sense of gratitude.

"The most beautiful thing we can experience is the mysterious."
—Albert Einstein

☛ Try This: Seek a Spark of Awe

Uncover the beauty around you. This practice guides you to embrace awe—take these steps with a curious heart.

Spot the Wonder (3 min.)

Look around for something awe-inspiring (e.g., nature, music, a kind act). What catches my eye or heart today?

Soak It In (4 min.)

Spend a few moments fully absorbing it—breathe deeply, let it sink in. *Example: Watch clouds drift or listen to a favorite song.*

Carry the Feeling (2 min.)

Note how awe shifts your mood and carry that lightness forward. How does this wonder linger?

Reflect & Write

- How could embracing wonder shape my day?
- What might block the feeling of awe in my day?

Quick Tip

Take an "awe walk" once a week to spark wonder.

For Further Exploration

Book: *The Book of Awesome* by Neil Pasricha – A celebration of life's small wonders.

Podcast: *The Wonder Dome* – Episodes on awe and inspiration.

Try It: Spend five minutes daily noticing something beautiful.

Trail Marker: Awe awaits—step into its quiet embrace.

10
A Final Act of Grace

Peace for You, Clarity for Them

Death is messy, but planning your wishes is a quiet love letter to those left behind—and a brave step toward peace with your own mortality. In this gentle act, you weave a thread of care that lingers beyond your days. It's a kind of spiritual housekeeping—making space for calm in both your life and theirs.

Why This Matters

We shy away from it, but facing end-of-life planning isn't just a gift to others—it's a spiritual release for you. That quiet fear of impermanence can weigh on your soul, yet confronting it with intention brings peace and purpose. Research shows that end-of-life planning reduces caregiver stress by 30% *(Journal of Palliative Medicine, 2020)*, easing the burden on loved ones while lightening your heart.

"We have a responsibility to shape our own stories. To shape our end as much as we shape our beginning."
—Atul Gawande

☛ Try This: Shape Your Legacy

Begin crafting your legacy today. This practice walks you through meaningful steps—take them with care and intention, allowing space to face your fears with love. Write your answers to the following and share them with someone you trust.

Logistics and Legacy (10 min.)

- Do you have a written will, trust, or letter of instruction?
- Have you let anyone know where these documents are?
- Have you set aside funds for final arrangements?
- Who should be notified and how?
- Have you completed a living will or advance directive?
- Who do you trust to make decisions if you can't speak for yourself? *Example: "Cremated, with ashes by the lake; my sister decides if I can't."*

Design a Ceremony (3 min.)

- Do you want a traditional funeral, a celebration of life, or a private gathering?

- Do you want to be buried or cremated?
- Do you prefer clothing, location, urn, or casket?
- Where would you like your body or ashes to rest?
- Is there music, a poem, a reading or a location that matters to you? *Example: "A quiet gathering with my favorite song; will is with my lawyer."*

Leave a Message (2 min.)

Is there anything you want to leave behind—words, letters, videos, blessings, apologies, or memories?

Reflect & Write

- What peace came from planning? What's still unclear?
- What decisions would I want to be made for me versus by me?

Quick Tip

Start with one wish and build from there.

For Further Exploration

Book: *Being Mortal* by Atul Gawande – Insights on the end of life.

Podcast: *Death, Sex & Money* – Episodes on legacy.

Try It: Write a one-page legacy letter this week.

Trail Marker: Grace lingers in the plans you leave behind.

11 Practicing Gratitude

Cultivating Joy Through Noticing

Gratitude turns the everyday into a quiet celebration of what's already here. It's not about big breakthroughs—it's about building a lens for wonder. Even small thank-yous whispered to no one in particular can gently rewire how you experience your days. Gratitude is a quiet rebellion against numbness.

Why This Matters

It's simple yet powerful—gratitude shifts your gaze to life's gifts. Studies show it can boost mental health by 25% *(UCLA Mindfulness Research, 2021).* Gratitude isn't just about making lists – it's about noticing that even on the hard days, something quietly good still wants to be seen.

> *"Gratitude turns what we have into enough."*
> *—Melody Beattie*

☛ **Try This: Build Your Gratitude Moment**

Set aside 5–10 minutes each evening to slow down and notice what was quietly good. Gratitude is like a muscle—the more you use it, the stronger and more natural it becomes.

Choose Your Way (3 min.)

Pick a format (e.g., notebook, phone, Five-Minute Journal) for evening reflection. What would I actually use?

Note Three Joys (4 min.)

Write three small moments from your day.

Example: "A laugh you shared; the way sunlight warmed your shoulders; a song that lifted your mood."

Feel the Warmth (2 min.)

Close your eyes, breathe in, and let each moment land. What do I feel when I let that memory back in?

Reflect & Write

- How might noticing gratitude change the way I move through my day?
- What might I miss if I don't notice?

Quick Tip

Try this nightly—small sips build a habit.

For Further Exploration

Book: *The Gratitude Diaries* by Janice Kaplan – A journey into gratitude.
Podcast: *Good Life Project* – Episodes on everyday joy.
Try It: Use the Five-Minute Journal for a week.

Trail Marker: Gratitude blooms where you pause to see.

---

12 Reclaiming Self

Remember Who You Are

When the roles you've lived inside begin to shift—through retirement, care giving, or loss—it's natural to feel a little untethered. The old structures fall away, and something quieter is revealed. This is your invitation to reconnect with the identity beneath the roles—the part of you that was never defined by a title.

Why This Matters

There's a moment when the nameplate comes down, the calendar clears, or the kids stop needing you—and suddenly, the person you were feels harder to find. Psychologist Dan McAdams calls this your narrative identity—the story you tell yourself about who you are. When that story gets blurry, so can your sense of peace and purpose. Rediscovering yourself beneath the titles isn't about going backward—it's about remembering what was always yours.

"The privilege of a lifetime is to become who you truly are."
- Carl Jung

☛ Try This: Go One Layer Deeper

Reflect on a time when you felt truly yourself, or recall a role that once defined you. If you completed the "The Life That's Most You" reflection in Chapter 1, consider revisiting it for added depth. Let's uncover your essence with these steps:

Circle One Faded Role (3 min.)

Choose a role you once found meaningful—parent, teacher, leader, caregiver.

Ask: What Did That Role Awaken in Me? (4 min.)

Was it creativity? Calm? Drive? Compassion? Name 2–3 qualities that came alive in you during that time.

Extract the Essence (2 min.)

Write one sentence that captures what's still alive in you—even if the role has changed. *Example: "Even though I'm no longer leading a team, I still carry the instinct to guide and encourage others."*

Reflect & Write

- What part of me have I set aside?
- What would it feel like to welcome that part back?

Quick Tip

Sometimes reclaiming starts with a simple "remember when..." conversation with someone who knew you before the roles.

For Further Exploration
Book: *Falling Upward* by Richard Rohr – On the second half of life and the deeper self.
Try It: Spend a week on morning pages (a Julia Cameron practice you can Google) to listen for your unfiltered self.
Podcast: *On Being* – Look for episodes on identity and transitions.

Trail Marker: You were never just what you did. The essence of you is still here—quiet, steady, waiting to be remembered.

Pocket Notes: Your Space to Reflect and Grow

Your Thrive Compass pointed to Spiritual Meaning—now it's time to capture what you've found. Use your Thrive Journal to jot insights, questions, or next steps. No rules—just what feels true.

Insights to Reflect On

- What stood out to me most in this chapter?
- Where do I feel spiritually connected in my life today?
- What recent moment sparked awe, wonder, or quiet meaning?
- How do gratitude or presence show up in daily life?
- Which of my values feel most alive to me now?
- How would I define spiritual well-being, in my words?

Ideas to Explore

- Activities I'm curious about that nourish my spirit
- New practices like meditation, journaling, or stillness
- Ways to nurture connection with people or nature
- How my daily choices reflect (or drift from) my values
- One mindset shift I'm ready to gently lean into
- Beliefs or assumptions I'd like to revisit or reframe

Actions to Take

- A daily ritual I want to begin practicing now
- A reflection or gratitude habit I'm ready to start
- A relationship I'll nurture with more presence and care
- A simple act of letting go I'm ready to try
- Honor curiosity by exploring something new this month
- Welcome awe or meaning each day

Chapter Four

Mental Clarity – The Mind's Role in Thriving

If your Thrive Compass nudged you toward this chapter, chances are your mind is asking for a little more calm—or at least a break from running in circles. Maybe it feels like your thoughts are playing bumper cars. Maybe your focus drifts, your memory fogs, or your brain is doing that thing where it reminds you of something embarrassing from 2004 right when you're trying to relax.

Whatever brought you here, this chapter is about reclaiming your mental space. Whether you're craving sharper attention, more presence, or just a little less chaos between the ears, you're in the right place.

The Quick Start guide below will help you quiet the noise, clear the mental desk, and find some breathing room inside your own head—no meditation app subscription required.

QUICK START

How to Use This Chapter

📖 Step 1: Start with "Mapping the Terrain."
Get a feel for why mental well-being matters and how it weaves into your thriving life.

👁 Step 2: Explore "What Great Looks Like."
Scan the statements in this section. Note when something resonates or sparks recognition.

🔔 Step 3: Reflect on "Warning Signs."
Move to the "Warning Signs" section. Scan and note any that feel familiar, even if it's just a small tug of recognition.

🔍 Step 4: Pinpoint "Possible Causes."
In this section, gently explore the list. Notice any that resonate with your current experience.

🛠 Step 5: Try "Remedies."

Use the Possible Causes you reflected on as a guide. Turn to the corresponding Remedies to find practical, actionable steps you can take to enhance your mental well-being.

Throughout, use the Pocket Notes prompts at the end of the chapter to reflect, capture insights, and shape any small next steps that feel meaningful to you.

🕮 Mapping the Terrain

Let's talk about your mind—it's where you live, and frankly, the landlord can be a little eccentric. Mental well-being isn't just about crossword puzzles and remembering where you left your glasses; it's about clarity, adaptability, and having enough curiosity to make life interesting.

In retirement, your brain loses the scaffolding of schedules and deadlines, which is freeing—until you realize you have to build the scaffolding yourself. This is your moment to feed it new challenges, spark it with fresh ideas, and occasionally give it the quiet it needs to connect the dots.

Think of it as keeping your mental tour guide caffeinated and curious. "My Own Journey" shares what happens when that guide has to find a new route. In the pages ahead, we'll explore ways to sharpen your focus, stretch your thinking, and keep your mind in shape for all the adventures—and misplaced keys—still to come.

My own journey:

I've always struggled with setting priorities. Jim, ever the pragmatist, would remind me, "If everything's important, then nothing is important," and "Perfection is the enemy of good enough." And I, ever the overachiever, would nod along while secretly thinking, "Yeah, but what if I just try a little harder?"

Turns out, Jim was right. (Don't tell him I said that.) What I didn't realize then—and still have to remind myself of now—is how easy it is to get stuck in a cycle of doing instead of deciding. I used to think prioritization meant figuring out how to do everything as efficiently as possible. Now I understand it's about choosing what actually deserves my time in the first place.

Retirement made this even trickier. With no set schedule, the days stretched out before me like a blank page—full of possibility, but also full of distractions. It's shockingly easy to spend an entire day feeling busy without actually accomplishing anything meaningful. That's where the "Clear & Keep" Method came in—a simple tool that forces me to sort out what's urgent, what's important, and what I can (gasp) let go of entirely. You'll find more on that later in this chapter, along with other strategies for sharpening focus, managing mental energy, and making space for what really matters.

And that's the thing about mental well-being—it's not about doing more, it's about doing what matters. So, what's one shift you could make today to bring more clarity or purpose into your mental space? The next few pages will help you distill where to focus, how to declutter your thinking, and how to keep your mind engaged and thriving. The good news? You're in the driver's seat.

👁 What Great Looks Like

Here's what mental well-being feels like when it's sharp and steady. These qualities aren't about being brilliant but noticing what's already clear or where a small tweak could lift the haze. Scan and note any that click.

- Stays focused without fraying.
- Sets clear goals and priorities.
- Tackles problems calmly.
- Decides without waffling too long.
- Keeps curiosity alive.
- Embraces learning and change.
- Nurtures creative imagination.
- Dreams up fresh solutions.

Notice where clarity, curiosity, or creativity already light up your mind—and imagine how a small pause could make them shine brighter.

🔔 Warning Signs

These are gentle nudges that your mind might need a little care, like a phone battery blinking red. They're not about guilt—just a chance to listen with curiosity. Jot what rings true in your notebook.

- Struggles to stay focused.
- Hesitates over decisions.
- Feels overwhelmed by basics.
- Lacks creative spark.
- Mood swings hit often.
- Feels stuck in a rut.
- Notices slower thinking.
- Feels bored or uninspired
- Has trouble staying organized.

These signs are just your mind whispering for a little TLC—time to listen and reconnect.

Possible Causes

Mental fog can creep in gradually, making it hard to notice. The table below helps name what may be clouding your thinking by pairing common Causes with targeted Remedies. Note any Cause that resonates, then turn to the corresponding Remedy in the next section. Brief explanations below the table offer more context if needed.

Causes	Remedies
Unskilled at setting goals	1. Set a Mental Challenge
Difficulty setting priorities	2. Clear the Clutter
Lack of purpose	3. Create a Personal Project
Overcommitment	4. Set Boundaries
Stuck in the past	5. Nurturing Curiosity for Greater Growth
Feeling stuck or discouraged	6. Reframing Challenges as Growth
Grieving a loss	7. Practicing Self-Care
Physical ailment	8. Body First

Causes with Explanations

Unskilled at setting goals

If your days feel more like a drift than a journey, it might be a sign that goal-setting isn't your strong suit right now. Without clear goals, it's easy to lose focus and feel unproductive, even when you're busy.

➔**See Remedy 1: Set a Mental Challenge** — *Recharging Your Focus and Energy* for practical ways to define what you want and create a sense of direction.

Difficulty setting priorities (a sense that 'everything is important')

When everything feels equally urgent, it's hard to know where to start. This inability to prioritize can leave you spinning your wheels and accomplishing little, even with the best of intentions.

➔**See Remedy 2: Clear the Clutter** — *Keep What Matters* to help you sort through the noise and focus on what truly matters most.

Lack of purpose

When life slows down or major roles shift, it's common to feel mentally adrift—like your days are passing without direction. But purpose doesn't have to be lofty or abstract. Often, a hands-on project with personal meaning can spark forward momentum.

➔**See Remedy 3: Create a Personal Project** — *Reignite Momentum Through Meaningful Doing* to shift from mental drift to meaningful motion.

Overcommitment

If your calendar looks like it's still working overtime, you might be struggling with overcommitment. Taking on too much can stretch your mental capacity thin, leaving little room for rest or reflection.

➔**See Remedy 4: Set Boundaries** — *Protect Your Time and Energy* to scale back and protect your mental well-being.

Stuck in the past

Dwelling on what was—whether it's career accomplishments, past mistakes, or old routines—can prevent you from fully embracing the present. Ruminating keeps you tethered to yesterday instead of building new experiences today.
➔**See Remedy 5: Nurturing Curiosity for Greater Growth** — *Unlocking New Passions and Perspectives* to help you step into new ideas that spark joy and energy.

Feeling stuck or discouraged

Sometimes life throws challenges that make you question your progress or potential. These moments often signal that your mindset—not your ability—needs renewal.
➔ **See Remedy 6: Reframing Challenges as Growth** — *Seeing Obstacles as Teachers* to learn how to transform setbacks into insight and rebuild confidence from the inside out.

Grieving a loss

Experiencing loss—whether of a loved one, a role, or a sense of identity—can weigh heavily on your mental well-being. The inner landscape can feel fragile or uncertain after major shifts.
➔**See Remedy 7: Practicing Self-Care** — *Tending the Heart During Hard Times* to process loss with compassion and rebuild resilience.

Physical ailment

When your body isn't cooperating, it's hard to focus on much else. Physical strain often creates a feedback loop of mental stress, fatigue, and diminished clarity.
➔**See Remedy 8: Body First** - *A Rescue Protocol for Your Brain* to prioritize energy and take small steps toward mental and physical recovery.

Remedies

🛠 This is your toolbox of practical, heartfelt steps to recharge your mind, sharpen focus, and spark curiosity. Pick remedies based on the causes that resonate in the previous section, or try any that tug at you, like a good idea over morning coffee. Jot insights in your journal.

Recharging Your Focus and Energy

1
Set a Mental Challenge

Your brain loves a little resistance. Without something to stretch toward, your thoughts can feel like they're drifting in circles. A small challenge—just engaging enough—can wake up your mind, sharpen focus, and return that sense of mental spark.

Why This Matters

When left unstimulated, the brain can slip into autopilot, making everything feel flat or forgettable. Research shows that setting and completing modest mental goals improves cognitive flexibility and short-term memory *(National Institute on Aging, 2022)*. Mental vitality isn't built through grand achievements—it's shaped by small, intentional challenges repeated over time.

"A goal without a plan is just a wish." — Antoine de Saint-Exupéry

☛ **Try This: Create Your SMART Mini-Mission**

Think of this as setting a low-pressure but meaningful mental tune-up. Small doesn't mean trivial—it means doable, repeatable, and energizing.

Capture a Curiosity (3 min.)

Jot down an idea that excites you—perhaps reading a new book, painting weekly, crafting a blog, or creating an instructional YouTube video.

Shape Your Plan (4 min.)

Craft it with a little flair. Keep it SMART: specific (like "one blog post weekly"), measurable (track those posts), achievable (something doable), relevant (tied to what sparks you), and time-bound (say, a month). Write your SMART goal on a notecard or sticky-note and place it where you'll see it, like on your fridge.

Take a First Step (2 min.)

Try your challenge today—maybe a quick riddle, a sketch, or a blog draft. Reflect: *How does this small effort feel?*

Reflect & Write

- What part of my mind feels underused or under stimulated?
- How would engaging that part affect my mood or energy?

Quick Tip

Start smaller than you think. Success builds momentum faster than ambition.

For Further Exploration

Book: *Atomic Habits* by James Clear – A roadmap for building small habits that stick

Podcast: *The Huberman Lab* – Start with the episode on how the brain learns and rewires

Try It: For one week, try a 5-minute challenge—reading, puzzling, doodling, or exploring a new skill. Watch what shifts.

Trail Marker: Mental energy builds not from pressure, but from purpose. Let one small goal pull you forward.

2 Clear the Clutter

Keep What Matters

Picture curating a gallery of your day's priorities: you choose which tasks or commitments light you up and gently set the rest aside. By focusing on what truly matters, you weave a calmer rhythm into your days and make room for peace in your mind.

Why This Matters

When everything competes for your attention, nothing gets your best focus. Studies show that focusing on meaningful, high impact tasks boosts productivity, reduces stress, and increases your sense of control *(Journal of Organizational Behavior, 2021)*. Prioritizing isn't about doing more—it's about doing what matters most.

☛ **Try This: Sort What Stays, Clear What Drains**

Think of this as a mental attic sweep. You're not tossing everything—just sorting what still serves you from what's been weighing you down.

Brain-Dump the Noise (3 min.)

Jot down everything swirling in your head—tasks, chores, lingering thoughts. Don't organize it. Just get it out.

Sort Into Meaning (4 min.)

On a fresh page, draw three columns: Keep It (meaningful or energizing), Clear It (draining busywork), and Schedule It (important but not urgent). Place each item from your list into one column, guided by what feels true to you.

Act on the Essentials (2 min.)

Start one Keep It task, cross off one Clear It, and calendar one Schedule It. Clearing even a little mental space shifts your whole day.

"Most of us spend too much time on what is urgent and not enough time on what is important."
— Stephen R. Covey

Quick Tip

Before starting your day, ask: What actually deserves my energy today?

Reflect & Write

- How does mental clutter affect how I show up?
- What energizing task have I been putting off?

For Further Exploration

Book: *Essentialism* by Greg McKeown — A guide to living by design, not by default

Podcast: *The One Thing* with Geoff Woods — How to find your focus and protect it

Try It: Choose one morning this week to tackle your "Keep It" task first. Feel the shift.

Trail Marker: When you clear the noise, what matters most begins to rise.

3 Create a Personal Project

Reignite Momentum Through Meaningful Doing

A small act of creation can light up your days like nothing else. A personal project, no matter how modest, becomes a quiet invitation to rediscover what makes you feel alive and whole.

Why This Matters

Purpose often hides in the doing, not just the dreaming. Studies show that engaging in meaningful projects can boost psychological well-being by up to 25% and enhance intrinsic motivation *(American Psychologist, 2021)*. Whether it's a scrapbook, a garden bed, or a new skill, a personal project gives you a tangible way to reconnect with what makes you feel alive.

"The best way to find yourself is to lose yourself in the service of something larger." — Mahatma Gandhi

☛ Try This: Start a 10-Day Spark Project

This is your invitation to start a mini mission—a small, joyful project that reignites your sense of momentum. Here's how to begin.

Capture Your Curiosity (3 min.)

What's been tugging at you lately? Jot down one idea that sparks your interest—maybe organizing family photos, starting a blog, sketching a garden layout, tracing your genealogy, or curating a playlist of life-defining songs. No idea is too small.

Map Your Micro-Sprint (4 min.)

Plan a 7–10 day challenge with one tiny task each day. For example, scan five photos, write one paragraph, sketch one plant, or add three songs to your playlist. Keep it simple—think 5–15 minutes daily.

Launch and Look Back (2 min.)

Start today, even for five minutes. At the end of your sprint, reflect: What surprised me? What felt most alive? Where might this project take me next?

Quick Tip

Don't wait for inspiration to strike. Pick one small action and let the momentum build from there.

Reflect & Write

- What does my curiosity around this project tell me about what I'm longing for right now?
- When I imagine myself engaging in this project, what feels most alive?

For Further Exploration
Book: *The Creative Act* by Rick Rubin – A soulful guide to unlocking your creative spark through intentional action.
Podcast: *The Accidental Creative*, episode on "Small Projects, Big Impact" – Todd Henry shares how bite-sized creative work fuels energy and purpose.
Try It: Pick a 10-day project theme and set a daily 15-minute timer. Jot down one thing you notice each day.

Trail Marker: A single act of creation, no matter how small, can awaken a version of you that's ready to thrive.

Protect Your Time and Energy

4
Set Boundaries

Saying yes to everyone else can quietly dim your own light. Over time, your days start to belong to everyone but you. Setting boundaries isn't about shutting people out—it's about carving out space for what truly matters to you.

Why This Matters

Without clear boundaries, it's easy to feel stretched thin, resentful, or just plain exhausted. Research shows that strong boundary-setting habits reduce stress and boost emotional well-being by up to 30% *(Journal of Occupational Health Psychology, 2018)*. Learning to say no—or a kind "not now"—keeps your energy aligned with what lights you up.

☛ Try This: Sort Your Yeses and Nos

Your time and energy are precious. This exercise helps you decide what deserves your "yes" and what needs a

"If it's not a Hell Yeah, it's a no."
— Tim Ferriss

gentle "no."

List Your Loads (3 min.)

Jot down 4–6 things you regularly do for others (e.g., volunteering, helping a friend, running errands). Next to each, mark it if it feels energizing (+) or draining (-).

Pick Your Priorities (3 min.)

Review your list. Circle one energizing (+) commitment to keep and protect. Underline one draining (-) commitment to reduce or let go.

Set a Boundary

For your underlined draining commitment, practice saying no (e.g., "I'm focusing on other priorities right now"). Before agreeing to a new commitment, take a moment to reflect: Does this excite me, or am I saying yes out of habit or obligation? If it's not an enthusiastic "Hell Yeah," politely decline or delay. This keeps your focus on what truly matters.

Quick Tip

A kind "no" is a gift to yourself and others—it creates space for authentic yeses.

Reflect & Write

- What do I notice when I imagine saying a clear, kind "no"?
- What does honoring my energy reveal about what I value most?

For Further Exploration

Book: *Set Boundaries, Find Peace* by Nedra Glover Tawwab – A practical guide to protecting your time and energy with clarity and compassion.

Podcast: *We Can Do Hard Things, episode "How to Say No"* – Glennon Doyle explores saying no with grace and overcoming guilt.

Try It: Rate three commitments this week and practice saying a kind "no" to the biggest drain.

Trail Marker: Saying no isn't rejection—it's a quiet act of self-respect.

5 Nurturing Curiosity for Growth

Unlocking New Passions and Perspectives

A curious mind turns every day into an adventure. It keeps the edges of your life soft and your mind open to change. Following a spark of wonder, no matter how small, keeps your world expansive, your thoughts nimble, and your heart open to surprise.

Why This Matters

Wonder opens doors to a richer, more vibrant life. Research links curiosity to enhanced mental agility, greater life satisfaction, and increased resilience *(Harvard Health, 2022)*. By exploring new topics or rediscovering old passions, you spark growth and unexpected moments of joy.

"Curiosity is the wick in the candle of learning."
— William Arthur Ward

☛ **Try This: Run a Curiosity Experiment**

This is a playful nudge to let your mind roam. No need for mastery—just a few minutes to explore what intrigues you.

Choose Your Spark (3 min.)

Pick one thing that piques your interest—maybe AI basics, jazz chords, succulent care, or Korean recipes. Stuck? Think back to a moment from Chapter 1 when you felt alive and curious.

Try a Micro-Quest (5 min.)

Do one small action: watch a short video, sketch an idea, try a recipe, or search a term that's been nagging you. Keep it light—five minutes is enough.

Catch the Ripple (2 min.)

Jot down one surprise from your quest and one new question it sparked. Let that question guide your next step.

Quick Tip

Curiosity isn't about mastering something. It's about showing up to meet it.

Reflect & Write

- What surprised me about where my curiosity wandered?

- What childhood passions could I chase today?

For Further Exploration
Book: *A Curious Mind* by Brian Grazer & Charles Fishman – A lively exploration of how curiosity shaped a Hollywood producer's creative life.
Podcast: *Ologies* with Alie Ward, episode "Volcanology (VOLCANOES!)" – A fun, awe-filled dive into science and discovery.
Try It: Set a 10-minute timer this week to explore a curiosity. Note where your mind wanders.

Trail Marker: Curiosity doesn't require a plan. It just needs permission. Let your questions lead—and joy will follow close behind.

6 Reframing Challenges as Growth

See Obstacles as Teachers

No one asks for detours, disappointments, or days that test our patience. Yet those moments often do the quiet work of shaping who we're becoming. When we learn to see challenges as teachers rather than tormentors, frustration softens into clarity, and growth becomes less about striving and more about seeing ourselves differently.

Why This Matters

Life rarely delivers insight neatly packaged—it arrives disguised as friction. How we interpret that friction changes everything. Research on growth mindset shows that viewing setbacks as part of the learning curve strengthens resilience, sharpens focus, and calms reactivity *(Dweck, Psychological Science, 2020)*. In truth, the problem isn't always the problem, it's how we hold it. Reframing turns "Why me?" into "What's this showing me?" and restores a sense of steadiness and agency.

☛ Try This: The Two-Column Perspective Shift
This simple exercise helps you transform challenges

into teachers. By seeing both sides—the obstacle and the opportunity—you train your mind to spot growth even in the grit.

Gather Your Moments (5 min.)

Think back over the past week and jot down three to five situations that frustrated, disappointed, or challenged you. These don't have to be dramatic—small irritations count. Write each one in a left-hand column labeled *The Challenge.*

Flip the Frame (7 min.)

Next to each challenge, create a right-hand column labeled *The Growth View.* Ask yourself: *What might this experience be teaching me?* or *What quality is this helping me strengthen?* Translate each frustration into a quiet gain—patience, clarity, communication, boundaries, or grace.

Spot the Pattern (5 min.)

After you've reframed several examples, look for common threads. Are the same themes appearing? Note one insight you'll carry forward this week—something like, *I'm learning to pause before reacting or I'm stronger at setting limits than I realized.*

"Live as if you were to die tomorrow. Learn as if you were to live forever."
— Mahatma Gandhi

Quick Tip

Reframing isn't about denying difficulty, it's about changing your angle of vision. Keep a small notebook or digital note for your two columns, and revisit it each week. You'll start noticing growth where frustration used to live.

Reflect & Write

- What perspective or truth can I see now that I couldn't see in the moment?
- How might I remind myself, next time, that struggling and growth often arrive hand in hand?

For Further Exploration

Book: *The Obstacle Is the Way* by Ryan Holiday — A

modern classic on transforming setbacks into strength through perspective and discipline.
Podcast: *Ten Percent Happier* with Dan Harris, episode "The Art of Resilience" — A conversation about reframing adversity and building emotional steadiness through mindfulness.
Try It: Revisit your Two-Column notes at the end of the month. Circle the patterns that keep showing up and write a single sentence that sums up what life seems to be teaching you right now.

Trail Marker: Clarity often arrives disguised as challenge. When you give each moment a second look, life slowly rearranges itself into meaning.

7 Practicing Self-Care

Tending the Heart During Hard Times

Grief or big life shifts can leave you feeling raw, like the world is moving faster than your heart can follow. In those moments, even the smallest acts—resting, walking, feeding yourself well—can become quiet forms of healing. Self-care helps steady the ground beneath you.

Why This Matters

Self-care is a lifeline for tending grief and rebuilding your footing. Daily practices like stretching, journaling, or simply resting have been shown to reduce anxiety, ease depressive symptoms, and support emotional regulation *(Health Psychology, 2024)*. Beyond the science, it's a way of whispering: I still matter, even now.

☛ **Try This: Create a Self-Care Menu**

You don't need an elaborate routine—just a few small, flexible tools that meet you where you are.

Build Your Menu (3 min.)

Make three simple columns labeled Mind, Body, and Soul. Under each, jot down a few activities that help you reset.

Mind (for racing thoughts): journaling, reading, guided meditation

Body (for physical tension): stretching, deep breathing, a short walk

Soul (for low mood): listening to music, painting, calling a friend

Aim for 3–5 ideas per column. Keep it flexible—this is your toolkit, not a to-do list.

Check Your Mood (3 min.)

Not sure what you need today? Let your mood choose for you:

- Feeling anxious → pick something from **Mind**
- Feeling tense → pick something from **Body**
- Feeling drained → pick something from **Soul**

Take Ten (4 min.)

Choose one thing and do it for ten minutes. A walk, a song, a stretch—whatever soothes or steadies you.

"Healing takes courage, and we all have courage, even if we have to dig a little to find it."
— Tori Amos

Quick Tip

Write your self-care menu on a sticky note or save it in your phone. Make it easy to reach when the day feels heavy.

Reflect & Write

- What feeling is asking for care right now?
- What would it mean to treat myself with the compassion I'd offer a friend?

For Further Exploration

Book: *On Grief and Grieving* by Elisabeth Kübler-Ross & David Kessler – A tender, insightful guide through loss and emotional renewal

Podcast: *The SelfWork Podcast* by Dr. Margaret Rutherford, Ep. "You Deserve Self-Care, Not Self-Criticism" – Honest talk on showing up for yourself in hard times

Try It: Choose one act from your Self-Care list each morning for one week. Notice how your energy and outlook shift.

Trail Marker: You don't have to fix everything today. Just care for the part of you that showed up.

8 Body First

A Rescue Protocol for Your Brain

Some days, your brain feels foggy, your fuse is short, and everything seems just a little too much. Often, that's your body waving a red flag—low sleep, poor nutrition, or too much couch time can quietly hijack your mind. This isn't emotional burnout—it's a system glitch. Quick, physical resets can bring your brain back online.

Why This Matters

Mental clarity starts in the body. Even mild sleep loss, dehydration, or lack of movement can tank your mood and focus. Research shows that restoring these basics—sleep, food, movement, and light—can significantly improve cognitive performance and emotional regulation *(Sleep Foundation, 2025; Harvard Health, 2022)*. You don't need a full overhaul—just a targeted reset to get back in sync.

"Take care of your body. It's the only place you have to live." — Jim Rohn

☛ Try This: Run a Reset Check-In

This is a quick triage for those "off" days—when you're irritable, foggy, or weirdly tired. It helps you spot what's out of whack and course-correct fast.

Scan Your Basics (3 min.)

Ask yourself:

- **Sleep**: Did I get at least seven hours last night?
- **Movement**: Have I moved today (e.g., walk or stretch)?
- **Fuel**: Have I eaten something nourishing recently?
- **Light**: Have I stepped outside to get natural light?

Identify the one area most out of balance right now. Start here.

Make a Small Shift (3 min.)

Now take a targeted action based on what you noticed:

- Low on **sleep**? try a 10-minute nap or rest
- Not **moving**? take a brisk walk or simply stretch

- Low on **fuel**? eat a protein-rich snack or hydrate.
- Low on **light**: step outside for 15 minutes and just breathe.

Notice the Change (2 min.)

Afterward, pause. Jot down one word for how you feel. Even a small shift can ripple through the rest of your day.

Quick Tip

Save your four triage questions in your phone for a quick check-in when you feel off.

Reflect & Write

- Which pillar—sleep, movement, food, or light—needs my care most today?
- What's one tiny reset I can try when I feel stuck?

For Further Exploration

Book: *Why We Sleep* by Matthew Walker – A compelling dive into sleep's role in mental clarity and health.

Podcast: *Huberman Lab*, episodes on sleep or light exposure – Dr. Andrew Huberman shares science-backed tips for optimizing brain health.

Try It: Choose one pillar (sleep, movement, food, light) and make a micro-upgrade today: go to bed 15 minutes earlier, take a brisk walk, pick a nutrient-rich snack, or spend five minutes in morning sun. Note the shift in your mood.

Trail Marker: A small act of care for your body can lift the fog and bring you back to yourself.

Pocket Notes: Your Space to Reflect and Grow

Your Thrive Compass pointed to Mental Well-Being—now it's time to capture what you've found. Use your journal or notebook—any one you love—to jot insights, questions, or next steps. No rules, just what feels true.

Insights to Reflect On

- What hit home in this chapter?
- Where do I feel sharpest in my mental well-being?
- Which habits boost my clarity or resilience?
- When does my mind feel most open or flexible?
- How would I define "mental well-being" in my own words?

Ideas to Explore

- Practices I'm curious about (e.g., mindfulness, journaling).
- Ways to weave learning or creativity into my days.
- Small routines for clarity (e.g., rest, boundaries).
- Mindsets to nurture (e.g., curiosity, patience).
- Old fears or habits I'm ready to rethink.

Actions to Take

- One daily habit to keep my mind clear.
- A new skill or hobby I'm excited to try.
- One boundary to protect my energy.
- A quick reset for when I'm stuck.
- How I'll celebrate small mental wins this month.

Chapter Five

Social Connection – The Power of Relationships

If your Thrive Compass led you here, your social life might need a little refresh—or, let's be honest, a major reboot. Maybe you're feeling a bit out of sync with old friends. Maybe you're wondering how to meet new people now that work no longer provides instant colleagues and awkward birthday cake in the breakroom. Or maybe you just miss having someone who texts you memes and remembers your dog's name.

Whatever brought you here, this chapter is about reconnecting—with others and with the part of yourself that craves real, human connection (yes, even if you're a proud introvert). Whether you're looking to rekindle old friendships, make new ones, or just deepen the relationships that bring meaning to your days, this is your starting point.

The Quick Start guide below will help you take stock of your current connections and begin crafting a social life that feels more like community and less like small talk at a networking event.

QUICK START

How to Use This Chapter

📖 **Step 1: Start with "Mapping the Terrain."**
Get a feel for why social well-being matters and how it roots you in a thriving life.

👁 **Step 2: Explore "What Great Looks Like."**
Scan the statements in this section. Note when something resonates or sparks recognition.

🔔 **Step 3: Reflect on "Warning Signs."**
Move to the "Warning Signs" section. Scan and note any that feel familiar, even if it's just a small tug of recognition.

🔍 **Step 4: Pinpoint "Possible Causes."**

In this section, gently explore the list. Notice any that resonate with your current experience.

🛠 **Step 5: Try "Remedies."**

Use the Possible Causes you reflected on as a guide. Turn to the corresponding remedy to find practical, actionable steps to enhance your social well-being.

Throughout, use the Pocket Notes prompts at the end of the chapter to reflect, capture insights, and shape any small next steps that feel meaningful to you.

🕮 Mapping the Terrain

Social well-being is the spark of feeling seen, heard, and understood. It's not about a packed contact list or a social calendar so full you need a personal assistant, it's the conversations that leave you lighter, the people who just get you. Retirement shakes up the social scene: no more watercooler chats or built-in colleagues. Without attention, solitude can sneak in like an uninvited guest. But here's the upside—you've got time to tend the relationships that matter and plant new ones.

Think of your social world as a garden. Some bonds are sturdy oaks, others need a trim, and fresh ones can bloom if you give them a little sunshine (and maybe a glass of wine). It's about belonging—to friends, family, or a community where you give as much as you get. Connection takes courage, patience, and the occasional "let's just do it" phone call, but it's what keeps you grounded.

What makes you feel part of something? Who's your go-to when life gets wobbly? This chapter invites you to nurture those ties, spark new ones, and build a circle that hums with meaning. "My Own Journey" below shares a story of rebuilding community from scratch—no RSVP required. From deeper friendships to the perfect "thinking of you" text, these pages offer ways to cultivate connection that lights you up.

My own journey:

When Jim and I moved to a new town after his retirement, we both hit the ground differently. He—ever the social butterfly—found a rhythm almost immediately. Fishing buddies, ski trips, impromptu lunches. Meanwhile, I was still figuring out where to buy milk and how to make small talk without sounding like I'd just been unfrozen from a glacier.

For me, connection has always taken time. When the kids were young, it felt easier—there was always a soccer game or school fundraiser to help strike up conversation. But in this chapter of life, there aren't as many built-in icebreakers. You have to create your own sense of community, which, for an introvert like me, meant learning to treat socializing with the same intention I once gave to organizing fundraisers and birthday parties.

What I eventually realized is that friendships in this season of life don't just show up at your door with a casserole. You have to be more mindful—more intentional. The goal-setting exercise in this chapter helped me take that first step. Writing my social vision statement made me realize two things: (1) I already have a handful of friendships I deeply value, even if they're now scattered across the map, and (2) I want to find kindred spirits locally—not just people to chat with, but people who light me up a little.

That clarity nudged me to join a running group and a local writing circle—two spaces where shared interest feels like solid ground. I won't say I've found my new BFF (not yet), but I have found warmth, curiosity, and real connection. And I trust that with time—and a little showing up—the roots will grow deeper.

That's the thing about social well-being—it isn't about collecting acquaintances or forcing connections. It's about knowing what you need, staying open to possibility, and planting seeds even when the garden still feels a little empty. As you move through this chapter, notice what kinds of connection feel most energizing to you and where you might take one small step to invite more belonging into your life.

👁 What Great Looks Like

Here's what social well-being feels like when it's blooming. They're not goals to chase, but signposts of what's possible with a little tending. Scan these qualities, noting in your journal any that spark a quiet "yes."

- Nurtures close bonds.
- Listens with care.
- Shares support freely.
- Joins in with ease.
- Speaks openly and respectfully, even in conflict.
- Expresses appreciation and gratitude for others.
- Nurtures meaningful relationships.
- Is open to new connections and social circles.

Notice where your connections already nourish you—and where a small new reach might invite even deeper belonging and joy.

Warning Signs

These gentle signals suggest your social world might need a little care. Scan the list, jotting in your notebook any that feel familiar, even faintly. They're invitations to tend to your connections with kindness.

- Spends little time interacting.
- Keeps others at a distance.
- Declines invitations more often than not.
- Spends more time alone than intended.
- Loses interest in social activities once enjoyed.
- Struggles with social norms and expectations.
- Neglects relationships without meaning to.
- Snaps in social settings.
- Feels stagnant and disconnected.
- Clings to routine to avoid change.

These signs are your inner compass hinting it's time to reach out, open up, and let connection grow again.

Possible Causes

Social disconnection can build quietly, making it easy to overlook. The table below helps name what may be influencing your sense of connection by pairing common Causes with supportive Remedies. Note any Cause that resonates, then turn to the corresponding Remedy in the next section. Brief explanations below the table offer more context.

Causes	Remedies
More interested in tasks than in people	1. Knowing Your Style
Low social confidence	2. Building Ease
Prefers solitude as an introvert	3. Honoring Solitude
Adjusting to a new community	4. Finding Belonging
Coping with the loss of a relationship	5. Healing After Loss
Lacks social goals	6. Setting Intentions
Struggling with illness, pain, or fatigue	7. Managing Energy
Feeling the pinch of financial constraints	8. Creating Options
Past social hurts	9. Releasing Baggage
Relies on social crutches for social ease	10. Embracing Truth

Causes with Explanations

More interested in tasks than in people

If crossing chores off your list feels easier than making small talk, your natural mode may be "do" rather than "chat." Knowing your style can help you connect without neglecting what fuels you.

➔**See Remedy 1: Knowing Your Style:** *Navigate Relationships Like a Seasoned Traveler* to sync your style and spark connection.

Low social confidence

When worries about saying the wrong thing overshadow the moment, social time can feel draining instead of fun. A touch of self-doubt is normal, but it doesn't have to steer the whole exchange.

➔**See Remedy 2: Building Ease**—*Turn Self-Doubt into Confidence* to help you feel more at ease as you step back into social interactions.

Prefers solitude as an introvert

If solitude leaves you energized, there's no need to force a crowd. It only becomes a concern when time alone starts to feel like loneliness instead of choice.

➔**See Remedy 3: Honoring Solitude** — *Thrive as an Introvert* for ways to nurture meaningful connections without losing the comfort of your own space.

Adjusting to a new community

Even the most outgoing soul can feel like a wallflower in a room full of strangers. Without a built-in welcome, finding your circle can feel like trial and error.

➔**See Remedy 4: Finding Belonging**—*Build Connections in a New Community* will help you take that first step with confidence and ease.

Coping with the loss of a relationship

When someone leaves—through distance, a falling-out, or loss—the space they held in your world can be hard to fill. Pulling back is natural, but connection can be part of the healing.

➔**See Remedy 5: Healing After Loss**—*Find Your Way Back to Others* offers a gentle path to help you re-enter the world of connection at your own pace.

Lacks social goals

Without a clear sense of what you want, friendships can quietly drift into the margins. Social well-being grows best when you set intentions for how connection fits your life.

➔**See Remedy 6: Setting Intentions** — *Create a More Connected Life* to define what meaningful connection looks like now and take purposeful steps toward it.

Struggling with illness, pain, or fatigue

When you're not feeling your best, socializing can feel like one more demand on already low energy reserves. If you've been turning down plans because the idea of going out sounds exhausting, physical well-being might be affecting your social engagement.

➔**See Remedy 7: Managing Energy** — *Stay Close on Tired Days* for gentle ways to maintain meaningful connection, even when your body needs rest and recovery.

Feeling the pinch of financial constraints

Good company doesn't require a big tab. If money worries keep you from saying yes, connection can still thrive in simple, low-cost gatherings that carry the same joy.

➔**See Remedy 8: Creating Options** — *Keep Friendships Fresh on a Budget* for smart, wallet-friendly ways to keep the good company flowing, the conversations lively, and your social life feeling rich in all the ways that matter.

Past social hurts

We've all had that friendship that ended with more questions than answers or a group where we never quite fit. Old wounds can shadow new opportunities until they're named and released.

➔**See Remedy 9: Releasing Baggage** — *Let Go to Make Room for What's Next* to examine what you're carrying, so you can begin to shed old stories and open space for more nourishing, present-day relationships.

Relies on social crutches for social ease

Leaning on a drink or a screen can feel like a shortcut to comfort, but often it creates more distance than closeness. Authenticity, not props, builds lasting connection.

➔**See Remedy 10: Embracing Truth** — *Find Connection Without the Crutch* to rediscover the ease of connecting without a buffer.

Remedies

🛠 This section offers practical steps to help you reconnect, deepen relationships, and feel more rooted in community. Pick remedies tied to the causes you noted or try any that spark curiosity. Jot insights in your journal, letting small actions bloom into lasting connection.

1

Knowing Your Style

Navigate Relationships Like a Seasoned Traveler

Retirement's social map can feel like a new city—exciting, full of possibilities, and easy to get lost in. Just like travelers, each person moves through social spaces with their own rhythm, speed, and style. Noticing your own social rhythm, and recognizing others', makes it easier to connect without losing yourself along the way.

Why This Matters

When you naturally match how someone communicates, whether it's their pace, tone, or way of expressing themselves, it helps the conversation flow and builds an easy sense of trust. In fact, studies show this simple kind of mirroring can boost connection by up to 30% *(Journal of Social Psychology, 2023)*. As your old routines shift in retirement, this awareness can make it easier to form genuine friendships without feeling like you have to overextend yourself.

☛ **Try This: Chart Your Social Compass**

Knowing your style—and spotting someone else's—sharpens two key skills of emotional intelligence: self-awareness and empathy. This quick activity helps you read the "social map," adjust your route, and make interactions flow like a well-planned trip.

Spot Your Style (2 min.)

Which style feels most like you? Pick a primary and secondary.

- **Trailblazer**: Direct, likes to-the-point communication.

- **Festival-Goer**: Lively, loves group energy and storytelling.
- **Steady Wanderer**: Calm, prefers deep, one-on-one talks.
- **Thoughtful Navigator**: Analytical, likes data-driven exchanges.

Map Their Style (3 min.)

Think of a friend or family member. What's their style? Write their name and style(s). How do your styles align or clash? For example, your Trailblazer directness might rush a Steady Wanderer's slower pace.

Adjust Your Style (2 min.)

Pick one way to match their style today:

- When speaking with a **Trailblazer**: Be concise, focus on goals.
- When speaking with a **Festival-Goer**: Match their energy, share a story.
- When speaking with a **Steady Wanderer:** Slow down, listen deeply.
- When speaking with a **Thoughtful Navigator:** Offer details, give time to reflect.

The best conversations feel like a shared rhythm. You don't need to change your destination—just fine-tune your approach to make the ride smoother for both of you.

"The most basic of all human needs is the need to understand and be understood."
– Ralph G. Nichols

Quick Tip

Jot your social style and a close friend's in your phone's notes for quick reference before meetups.

Reflect & Write

- Who do I connect with effortlessly, and why might our styles align?
- Where do I feel friction in conversations, and how could adjusting my style help?

For Further Exploration
Book: *People Styles at Work...and Beyond* by Robert Bolton & Dorothy Bolton – A guide to behavioral styles for better communication.
Podcast: *Hidden Brain*, episodes on social dynamics – Shankar Vedantam explores how we connect and misconnect.
Try It: For one week, note one person's social style daily (e.g., at a coffee shop or club). Adjust your approach slightly and notice the difference. Practice makes perfect.

Trail Marker: Adapting your social style can turn strangers into allies, and conversations into connections.

2
Building Ease

Turn Self-Doubt into Confidence

Some people stride into a room like they own the place; others slip in hoping not to be noticed. If you're in the second camp, don't worry—ease in social settings isn't a fixed trait, it's a skill you can grow. With the right small steps, you can teach your brain to feel at home in conversation.

Why This Matters

Confidence shapes how others see you and how you see yourself. When you practice low-pressure interactions, your brain builds new patterns that make future conversations feel less daunting. Research shows that repeated positive interactions can rewire social anxiety into social comfort *(Clinical Psychology Review, 2020).*

☛ **Try This: The Confidence Ladder**

Think of this as climbing a ladder—you don't start at the top, you take it rung by rung. Each small interaction strengthens your footing and makes the next step easier.

Start on the Ground Floor (3 min.)

Offer a warm hello to someone you pass, or make brief eye contact with a smile. Tiny wins set the tone for bigger ones.

Step Up to Small Talk (3 min.)

Make a light comment on something you share with the other person—like the weather, the coffee line, or the music playing.

Reach the Next Rung (3 min.)

Ask a simple, open-ended question *("What brings you here today?")* and listen for a natural point to continue the exchange.

"Each time we face our fear, we gain strength, courage, and confidence in the doing." – Eleanor Roosevelt

Quick Tip

Keep your first goal tiny—comfort grows faster when you give it room to breathe.

Reflect & Write

- When have I felt most at ease socially, and what helped?
- What's one small risk I can take to stretch my comfort zone this week?

For Further Exploration

Book: *The Charisma Myth* by Olivia Fox Cabane – A practical guide to presence and confidence in any social setting.
Podcast: *The Science of Happiness* – Episodes on building confidence through connection.
Try It: Commit to three low-stakes interactions this week. Notice if the second feels easier than the first.

Trail Marker: Confidence isn't a sudden leap—it's the quiet stacking of small, steady wins.

3 Honoring Solitude

Thrive as an Introvert

If you love your alone time and find socializing exhausting, you're not broken—you're just wired differently. Some people thrive in the buzz of a crowd; others find their sweet spot in smaller, more meaningful exchanges.

Why This Matters

When you match your social life to your energy patterns, connection becomes something you look forward to rather than something you recover from. Research shows that honoring your natural temperament improves life satisfaction and relationship quality *(Personality and Social Psychology Bulletin, 2020).* This approach helps you nurture relationships in a way that's sustainable and deeply rewarding.

"I hold this to be the highest task of a bond between two people: that each should stand guard over the other's solitude."
- Rainer Maria Rilke

☛ Try This: The Introvert's Social Blueprint

This quick blueprint helps you pinpoint what feeds your energy, what drains it, and how to shape your calendar so you get more of the first and less of the second.

Identify What Energizes You (2 min.)

Circle or jot the ones that fit:

- One-on-one conversations over coffee
- Small gatherings with close friends
- Shared activities (hiking, book club, volunteering)
- Short, purposeful virtual check-ins (texts, voice notes)

Pinpoint What Drains You (2 min.)

Circle or jot the ones that fit:

- Large, noisy events
- Long social stretches without breaks
- Constant small talk
- Unstructured gatherings with mostly strangers

Shape Your Week (2 min.)

Choose one adjustment for the next 7 days:

- Say yes only to what feels energizing
- Block quiet time after social events
- Set gentle boundaries ("I can join for an hour")

Quick Tip

You're not avoiding people—you're protecting the quality of your presence.

Reflect & Write

- When have I felt most at ease socially?
- How can I share my need for recharge time without guilt?

For Further Exploration
Book: *Quiet: The Power of Introverts in a World That Can't Stop Talking* by Susan Cain – Explores the strengths of introverts and how to thrive in an extrovert-oriented world.
Podcast: *The Introvert,* Dear Podcast – Offers practical tips and relatable stories for navigating life and relationships as an introvert.
Try It: Swap one draining social plan this week for one that better fits your energy.

Trail Marker: Connection blooms when you make room for the kind of interactions that make you want more, not less.

4 Finding Belonging

Build Connections in a New Community

Moving somewhere new can feel like the first day at a new school, except there's no homeroom teacher pointing out potential friends. Even if you're naturally outgoing, stepping into an established circle can feel like crashing someone else's dinner party. Small, intentional efforts—offering a smile, showing up again—can quietly open the door to something real.

Why This Matters

Loneliness isn't just uncomfortable—it's linked to higher rates of depression, anxiety, and even heart disease *(National Academies of Sciences, 2020)*. Even a few meaningful ties can lift your mood, boost resilience, and offer a sense of belonging. Approaching connection like a slow-cooked meal—steady, warm, and deeply nourishing—makes it sustainable.

☛ Try This: Map Your Way to New Connections
Think of this as scouting your landscape. Opportunities to connect often hide in plain sight. This exercise helps you notice them and take one step toward turning them into something real.
Find Your Connection Points (3 min.)

"A journey of a thousand miles begins with a single step."
— Lao Tzu

Write down 2–3 places or activities where people naturally gather in your area, like a local walking group, a library class, or your favorite coffee shop. These become your "friendly territory" where conversation can happen naturally.

Pick a Low-Pressure Opener (4 min.)

Choose one small action that feels doable: introduce yourself to a neighbor, strike up a brief conversation at the gym, or commit to attending a community event for just an hour. The goal is to make it easy to say yes.

Take One Step This Week (2 min.)

Schedule one of those actions into your calendar—yes, write it down. Treat it like any other important appointment, because connection deserves space too.

Quick Tip

You're not auditioning for a best friend role—just making room for the possibility.

Reflect & Write

- Where do I already feel a sense of ease with people?
- What kinds of interactions leave me feeling more like myself?

For Further Exploration

Book: *Together: The Healing Power of Human Connection in a Sometimes Lonely World* by Dr. Vivek Murthy – A thoughtful look at why connection matters and how to nurture it.

Podcast: *The Art of Making Friends as an Adult* – Practical, research-backed advice for building meaningful relationships.

Try It: Say yes to one invitation this week—or create your own by inviting someone for coffee or a walk.

Trail Marker: Belonging doesn't arrive all at once—it's built, one friendly moment at a time.

Find Your Way Back to Others

Loss rearranges the furniture in your life. One day, someone's there, sharing your table, your phone calls, your everyday shorthand and the next, the room feels too big. This isn't about "moving on" (who came up with that phrase, anyway?)—it's about carrying forward what mattered and making room for new connections, one small step at a time.

Why This Matters

Humans are wired for connection, and when loss cuts one of those threads, it can feel like your whole social fabric unravels. Research shows that rebuilding even a few social ties can reduce isolation and depression by up to 30% *(American Journal of Psychiatry, 2015).* This remedy helps you start sewing again—without feeling like you need to make a whole quilt overnight.

"The pain of grief is just as much a part of life as the joy of love... the price we pay for love."
— Dr. Colin Murray Parkes

☛ Try This: Honor What's Gone, Nurture What's Here

Grief and connection can live side by side. This reflection helps you honor what's missing while gently leaning into the relationships that remain within reach.

Name and Honor the Loss (3 min.)

Write down who or what is gone and what they brought into your life—comfort, laughter, encouragement, perspective. Seeing it on paper acknowledges the gap.

Reflect on Your Bright Threads (4 min.)

List one or two people who bring even a spark of warmth or connection. They don't have to be your new best friend—just someone who makes you feel a little more like yourself when you're around them.

Take One Gentle Step (2 min.)

Take a small step toward connection—send a "thinking of you" text, invite someone for coffee, or say yes to an invitation you might normally decline. You might also choose to reconnect with someone from your

"Life That's Most You" list in Chapter 1. You're not committing to a weekly standing date—just opening a door.

Quick Tip

Think of it as dipping a toe back in the social pool—you're not cannonballing.

Reflect & Write

- What does this loss ask me to release right now?
- Where do I notice myself closing off?
- What am I protecting?

For Further Exploration

Book: *Healing After Loss* by Martha Whitmore Hickman – Daily meditations that meet you gently where you are in the grieving process.

Podcast: *Grief Out Loud (The Dougy Center)* – Thoughtful stories and conversations that remind you you're not alone.

Try It: Send a "thinking of you" message to one person this week. No long explanation required—just a simple hello.

Trail Marker: You're not replacing what was lost, you're proving connection is still possible.

6
Setting Intentions

Create a More Connected Life

We set goals for our health, finances, and travel plans—but friendship? Most of us just wing it and hope something meaningful happens. Connection doesn't grow on autopilot.

Why This Matters

In retirement, your schedule may be more open, but meaningful relationships still require care and planning. Studies show that adults who intentionally cultivate social connections report higher life satisfaction and a 50% lower risk of early mortality *(Holt-Lunstad et al., 2010).*

> *"If you want to go far, go together."*
> *— African Proverb*

☛ **Try This: Map Your Social Compass**

Every journey benefits from a compass. Here you'll clarify the kinds of connections that matter most to you now, then choose one simple way to move in that direction.

Clarify Your Connection Vision (3 min.)

Write down when you feel most connected—like deep one-on-one talks, group projects, shared rituals. Also note what drains you. This gives you a personal map of where to focus your time.

Write It in a Sentence (4 min.)

Craft a short statement that captures your vision:

- "I want to rebuild two deep friendships I can count on."
- "I'd like to join a small group that meets monthly."
- "I want to spend more time with curious, warm people."

Take One Intentional Step (2 min.)

Pick something simple and low-pressure: invite someone for coffee, attend a local event, or set a reminder to check in with a friend weekly. You're not overhauling your social life—just opening the first door.

Quick Tip

Treat connection goals like any other goal: write them down, revisit them, and give them space on your calendar.

Reflect & Write

- What kind of connection am I craving right now?
- What small step could I take this month to bring more of it into my life?

For Further Exploration

Book: *Frientimacy by Shasta Nelson* – A guide to creating deeper, more satisfying adult friendships.

Podcast: *The Art of Friendship* with Kim Wier – Tools and conversations on building meaningful, lasting connections.

Try It: Write your Social Vision Statement and place it where you'll see it weekly—use it as your compass for how you spend your social energy.

Trail Marker: Connection grows where intention meets action.

7 Managing Energy

Stay Close on Tired Days

Some days, just putting on pants feels like an Olympic event. When illness, chronic pain, or fatigue steps in, even fun plans can feel like a marathon you didn't sign up for. This isn't about pushing through to exhaustion—it's about finding connection that meets you where you are, so you still feel part of the world without depleting yourself.

Why This Matters

Even light social contact—a short call, a friendly text, a shared smile—can lift mood, reduce isolation, and support recovery *(Holt-Lunstad, 2015).* The key is designing connection that adapts to your capacity, so you can stay socially nourished without running yourself ragged.

"What is essential is invisible to the eye." — Antoine de Saint-Exupéry

☛ Try This: Match Connection to Your Energy

Your social life doesn't have to ignore your energy level. This quick check-in helps you gauge how much you have to give today and match your connections to fit.

Gauge Your Energy (1 min.)

Ask yourself: *Where am I today?*

- *Green* – Feeling good; I can do something social and in person.
- *Yellow* – A little tired; I'm up for low-key, shorter, or smaller gatherings.
- *Red* – Running on fumes; I need quiet easy, connection.

Pick a Matching Connection (2–5 min.)

- *Green* - Meet for coffee, join a small gathering, or take a walk with someone.
- *Yellow* - Call a friend for 10–15 minutes, join a short online class, or write a thoughtful message.
- *Red* - Send a "thinking of you" text, share a photo or voice memo, or sit quietly with someone—no talking required.

Post Your Personal Menu (2 min.)

Keep your energy guide somewhere visible—on your fridge, in your journal, or as your phone lock screen. On low-energy days, it takes the decision-making off your plate.

Quick Tip

You don't have to be "on" to be connected—sometimes presence alone is enough.

Reflect & Write

- Who in my life feels easy and nourishing to be around?
- On my lowest days, how can I remind myself I'm still part of something bigger?

For Further Exploration

Book: *The Art of Rest* by Claudia Hammond – A research-based guide to the many forms of rest and how to find the kind that works for you.

Podcast: *The Happiness Lab* with Dr. Laurie Santos – Episodes exploring how even brief, low-energy connections can boost mood and well-being.

Try It: Create your own "Social Energy Menu" with low-, medium-, and high-energy connection ideas. Keep it handy for quick reference.

Trail Marker: Connection doesn't always mean going out—it means reaching out, in ways that work for you today.

Keep Friendships Fresh on a Budget

8 Creating Options

Friendship shouldn't feel like a luxury item. When money's tight, it's tempting to skip plans—not because you don't care, but because the "price of admission" feels too steep. The truth? Some of the best connections cost nothing more than your time and attention.

Why This Matters

Research shows that relationships, not income, are the strongest predictors of life satisfaction *(Harvard Study of Adult Development, 2023)*. When you remove the "price of admission" from friendship, you make connection more frequent, authentic, and sustainable.

"Friendships are built on the simplest moments shared with intention." - Morgan Harper Nichols

☛ Try This: Build Your Low-Cost Connection Menu

Think of this as stocking your social pantry. With a ready list of simple, affordable options, you'll always have something nourishing to offer when connection calls.

Spot What Feels Right (3 min.)

Think about the social moments that feel easy and joyful—whether it's a deep one-on-one chat, a small gathering, or a shared walk. Write down the styles of connection that suit you best.

Gather Free or Low-Cost Ideas (4 min.)

List activities that cost little or nothing—potlucks, walk-and-talks, game nights, book swaps, free community events, volunteering. Aim for at least five options you'd actually look forward to.

Extend a No-Pressure Invitation (3 min.)

Write down 1–3 people who'd be game for low-key get-togethers. Pick one name and send a warm, simple invite: *"Coffee at my place?" "Want to walk this weekend?" "Up for a game night?"* Lead with warmth, not your budget. (If you can't think of anyone right now, revisit Remedy 4: Finding Your People for ways to meet potential friends.)

Quick Tip

You don't have to mention the budget—just lead with the fun.

Reflect & Write

- What kinds of connection feel most meaningful to me right now?
- Is money truly the barrier or could I reframe what con-

nection looks like?
- Who in my life might welcome simpler, more intentional time together?

For Further Exploration

Book: *The Art of Frugal Hedonism* by Annie Raser-Rowland & Adam Grubb – A witty guide to living richly while spending less, full of ideas for joyful, low-cost living.

Podcast: *The Minimalists* – Conversations on living intentionally, focusing on what matters most, and finding connection beyond consumerism.

Try It: Choose one no-cost ritual—a weekly walk, a BYO-mug coffee morning, or a "thinking of you" text—and keep it going for a month.

Trail Marker: The best parts of friendship can't be itemized on a receipt.

9 Releasing Baggage

Let Go to Make Room for What's Next

Some memories you carry like a favorite scarf. Others? More like a sandbag. Letting go doesn't erase the story—it just stops it from narrating every scene.

Why This Matters

Lingering social wounds can subtly limit trust, warmth, and even your willingness to try again. Research shows that unresolved social stress can fuel isolation and make it harder to form new bonds *(Journal of Social and Personal Relationships, 2018)*. Releasing what no longer serves you creates room for healthier, more joyful connections to take root.

☛ Try This: The Social Reset — Keep What Lifts You, Drop What Weighs You Down

Every relationship leaves a trace. This reset helps you notice what still strengthens you—and what's ready to be set down—so you can travel lighter in your connections.

"Sometimes we just need to be reminded: Not everyone we lose is a loss."
— Unknown

Pinpoint the Moment (2 min.)
Write a quick recap of one past social experience that still echoes in your thoughts—just enough detail to capture what happened and why it stuck with you. Keep it to a few sentences so it stays focused.

Spot the Ripples (3 min.)
Ask yourself: *How did this shape my trust, my habits, or my willingness to connect?* Be honest, but don't relive every frame.

Choose Your Carry-On (3 min.)
Decide on one lesson, boundary, or strength you'll keep—and one belief or habit you'll release. Put the "keep" into practice this week in a small way, like sending a friendly note, saying yes to coffee, or speaking up for yourself.

Quick Tip

You can honor the lesson without keeping the whole suitcase.

Reflect & Write

- What past social experiences might still shape how I connect today?
- What do I want to carry forward—kindness, boundaries, courage?

For Further Exploration

Book: *Platonic* by Marisa G. Franco — A research-based, insightful guide to building and sustaining meaningful friendships at any age.

Podcast: *We Can Do Hard Things* — Episodes that explore friendship, forgiveness, and trust with humor, depth, and honesty.

Try It: Write a letter (you don't have to send it) to someone from your past—name what you needed, what you're releasing, and what you're keeping.

Trail Marker: Travel light—the best connections meet you where you are, not where you've been.

Find Connection Without the Crutch

10
Embracing Truth

Sometimes we carry more into a conversation than our words—like a glass, a phone, or the steady hum of a screen. These little go-tos can make social moments feel safer, but over time, they can quietly slip between us and the people we're with Noticing when the helper becomes the habit—and practicing presence without it—can open the door to deeper connection.

Why This Matters

Even passive distractions—like a silent phone on the table—can lower the quality of a conversation and leave both people feeling less connected *(Przybylski & Weinstein, 2013).* And social "props" like drinks or screens can become quiet habits that keep us from showing up fully. Setting these crutches aside sharpens your ability to read cues, respond authentically, and build the kind of trust that turns an ordinary chat into one of the best scenes in your story.

"The best gift you can give someone is your presence."
— Thich Nhat Hanh

☛ Try This: Spot Your Shortcut, Try Something New

We all reach for small crutches when we're uneasy. This exercise invites you to notice yours with compassion and gently experiment with a different way of showing up.

Name Your Social Shortcut (3 min.)

Jot down the habit you most often reach for when you feel uncertain—maybe it's holding your phone, topping up your glass, or busying yourself with a task. Name it clearly so you can recognize it in the moment.

Understand the Pull (4 min.)

Write 1–2 sentences about what that habit gives you—comfort, distraction, control, or escape. You're not shaming yourself; you're learning your pattern.

Try a Gentle Swap (3 min.)

Choose one low-stakes social moment this week to either skip your crutch entirely or use it with intention. Afterward, note what you felt, what helped you stay grounded, and what you noticed about your presence.

Quick Tip

Curiosity works better than willpower here—ask *"What happens if I try it this way?"* instead of *"I have to stop doing this."*

Reflect & Write

- When do I feel most present in conversation—and what helps me stay there?
- Is there a habit I lean on that might block deeper connection?

For Further Exploration

Book: *The Power of Now* by Eckhart Tolle – A practical, accessible guide to cultivating moment-to-moment presence in everyday life.

Podcast: *The Mindful Minute* by Meryl Arnett – Short, calming episodes on bringing more presence and less autopilot into your day.

Try It: In your next conversation, put your "prop" out of reach for five minutes. Notice how your attention shifts.

Trail Marker: Presence is not something you earn—it's something you allow.

❖ Pocket Notes: Your Space to Reflect and Grow

Your Thrive Compass pointed you toward Social Connection—and now you have a clearer sense of the relational landscape you're navigating. Pocket Notes are here to help you notice what's nourishing you socially, what might need shifting, and how you can build more intentional connections going forward.

Insights to Reflect On

- What stood out to me most in this chapter?
- With whom do I feel most grounded and genuinely myself?
- What roles or patterns am I rethinking socially?
- Which interactions bring joy, comfort, or energy?
- When do I feel a true sense of belonging?
- How do I define social well-being?

Ideas to Explore

- Rituals to deepen ties (e.g., weekly calls)
- Boundaries that protect energy
- People I've been meaning to reach out to
- Groups or spaces I'm curious to explore
- Creative ways to connect (e.g., walks, notes, shared projects)

Actions to Take

- One low-pressure way to nourish connection this week
- A friendship I want to nurture more intentionally
- A small act of kindness I'll offer someone
- A social habit I'm ready to shift
- One step toward mutual care in a relationship
- How I'll grow support and feel more connected

Chapter Six

Emotional Balance – Riding the Waves of Life

If your Thrive Compass nudged you here, your heart might be asking for a little more calm—or at least fewer surprise waves of worry, irritation, or inexplicable weepiness at random commercials. Maybe life's changes have left you feeling a bit unmoored. Maybe you're just wondering where all your joy wandered off to, and whether it's planning to return.

Whatever brought you here, this chapter isn't about forcing happiness or pretending you're fine when you're clearly not. It's about learning how to feel what you feel—without getting swept out to sea—and building the kind of emotional steadiness that keeps you grounded when things shift (because they always do).

The Quick Start guide below will help you take stock of how you're doing emotionally—and gently walk you toward more balance, resilience, and maybe even a little joy that sneaks up on you when you least expect it.

QUICK START

How to Use This Chapter

📖 **Step 1: Start with "Mapping the Terrain."**
Get a feel for why emotional well-being matters and how it weaves into your thriving life.

👁 **Step 2: Explore "What Great Looks Like."**
Scan the statements in this section. Note when something resonates or sparks recognition.

🔔 **Step 3: Reflect on "Warning Signs."**
Move to the "Warning Signs" section. Scan and note any that feel familiar, even if it's just a small tug of recognition.

🔍 **Step 4: Pinpoint "Possible Causes."**
In this section, gently explore the list. Notice any that reso-

nate with your current experience.

🛠 **Step 5: Try "Remedies."**

Use the Possible Causes you reflected on as a guide. Turn to the corresponding Remedy to find practical, actionable steps you can take.

Throughout, use the Pocket Notes prompts at the end of the chapter—or your own journal—to reflect, capture insights, and shape any small next steps that feel meaningful to you.

📖 Mapping the Terrain

Emotional well-being is the undercurrent that shapes how life feels day to day. Joy, love, and contentment bring the bright notes, while sadness, frustration, and fear carry the shadows. Retirement doesn't erase the tougher emotions—you'll still face health scares, shifting relationships, or the occasional day that simply falls flat. The key isn't dodging those feelings but meeting them in a way that keeps you steady enough to move forward.

How you handle emotions colors everything—how clearly you think, how easily you connect, even how well your body holds up under stress. Emotional well-being is less about "staying positive" and more about having tools that let you pause, breathe, and respond with intention instead of reacting on autopilot.

I first came across one of these tools back in grad school, and it's stuck with me ever since. It gave me a way to catch myself when things started to tip off balance—and to bring the melody back before the low notes took over. In "My Own Journey," I'll share how that simple perspective still shapes the way I ride out life's dips.

This chapter invites you to explore strategies that make space for both resilience and tenderness: ways to ride life's waves with balance, curiosity, and self-compassion. Because in the end, emotional well-being isn't about erasing the lows, but about weaving them into a richer, steadier score.

My own journey:

I first learned about the "emotional fever" rule over 30 years ago in grad school, and I didn't think much of it at the time. It was simple enough: if your mood feels off for a day or two, just take care of yourself—rest, reach out, or watch something that makes you laugh. But if that heaviness sticks around for more than three days, as with a physical fever, it's a signal to talk to someone you trust.

Back then, I probably shrugged and thought, Okay, makes sense. But over the years, that little guideline has quietly become one of the most useful companions I carry. Life has a way of serving up both the highs and the lows, and retirement only amplifies them. Without work to distract you, joy can feel bigger—but so can the quiet stretches that lean toward loneliness, worry, or just the blues that don't seem to lift.

I can't say I always followed the "rule" perfectly. Sometimes I brushed it aside, telling myself I should be able to just snap out of it. Other times I over corrected—panicking at a bad day and thinking something must be terribly wrong. But somewhere along the way, I realized it wasn't really a rule at all. It was more like a gentle guardrail. A reminder that emotions, like the weather, are supposed to shift.

These days, I try to treat it more lightly. I notice when the skies are cloudy, make a small adjustment—call a friend, step outside, let myself laugh at something silly—and wait for the sun to break through. And if it doesn't after a while, I know it's time to reach out. That shift in perspective has kept me from getting stuck, and it's helped me see that emotional well-being isn't about staying sunny all the time. It's about knowing when to grab an umbrella, and when to ask someone to walk beside you until the storm passes.

👁 What Great Looks Like

Here's what emotional well-being feels like when it's flowing smoothly. These qualities highlight what's possible—not to force balance, but to see what's already steady or where a gentle shift could deepen your peace. Jot down in your journal or notebook any that feel true or spark a quiet "yes" inside you.

- Stays calm under pressure.
- Laughs off small mishaps instead of spiraling down.
- Listens with warmth, even when tension runs high.
- Bounces back quickly from life's curveballs.
- Offers comfort without needing to fix everything.
- Releases grudges before they harden into stone.
- Trusts instincts and adapts with steady grace.
- Welcomes feedback without losing confidence.
- Finds calm in disagreements and softens the edges.
- Shows kindness generously, even when unnoticed.

Notice where emotional steadiness, compassion, and flexibility already live within you—and where small steps might help those strengths grow even deeper over time.

🔔 Warning Signs

These are gentle ripples that your heart might need a little care. They're not about blame—just an invitation to listen with kindness. Scribble in your journal or notebook any that tug at you.

- Snaps quickly and stays hot too long.
- Flips out over little things that don't matter.
- Feels wired and restless, even when all is calm.
- Withdraws into distance when connection would help.
- Refuses help, even when drowning inside.
- Digs in stubbornly, clinging to being right.
- Grabs for control when uncertainty creeps in.
- Sees catastrophe in every stumble or setback.
- Makes rash decisions that backfire fast.
- Struggles to soften, forgive, or let go.

Noticing these signs isn't about labeling yourself—it's about opening a doorway to greater calm, clarity, and emotional resilience.

Possible Causes

Emotional shifts can happen gradually, making them easy to overlook. The table below helps name what may be contributing to that imbalance by pairing common Causes with supportive Remedies. Note any Cause that resonates, then turn to the corresponding Remedy in the next section. Brief explanations below the table offer context if needed.

Causes	Remedies
Weak Impulse Control	1. Find Your Triggers
Uncomfortable with difficult feelings	2. Sit With It
Easily overwhelmed by stressors	3. Press Pause
Together all the time	4. Reset the Ratio
Harsh inner critic or self-doubt	5. Challenge the Tape
Perfectionistic tendencies	6. Loosen the Grip
Grieving a major loss	7. Tend the Wound
Overcommitted and emotionally depleted	8. Recalibrate
Feeling unseen or under-appreciated	9. Reclaim Your Worth
Struggling to manage emotional input	10. Filter the Noise
Physical pain or chronic health issues	11. Care for the Container
Leaning too heavily on emotions to make decisions	12. Balance the Scales

Causes with Explanations

Weak impulse control

Emotions sometimes surge before thought has a chance to catch up. You may find yourself reacting faster, louder, or sharper than you intended, like hitting "send" on a message before proofreading.

➔**See Remedy 1: Find Your Triggers** — *Recognize Patterns That Hijack Your Calm* for tools to pause, reflect, and choose a calmer response.

Uncomfortable with difficult feelings

Rather than sit with discomfort, you keep busy, power through, or numb out. Avoidance may feel easier in the moment, but emotions have a way of resurfacing—often louder and harder to ignore.
➔**See Remedy 2: Sit With It** — *Build Tolerance for Tough Emotions* to stay present when feelings get uncomfortable.

Easily overwhelmed by stressors

Too many demands can leave even small requests feeling like the final straw. Your emotional bandwidth shrinks, making perspective and calm harder to access.
➔**See Remedy 3: Press Pause** — *Use Micro-Breaks to Reset and Recenter* to rebuild breathing space into your day.

Together all the time (and it shows)

More time with your partner in retirement means habits once barely noticed—like throat-clearing or noisy snacking—can start to feel disproportionately irritating. The issue isn't the quirk itself, but the sheer frequency with which it now intrudes on your space, silence, or sense of control.
➔**See Remedy 4: Reset the Ratio** — *Use the 5:1 Rule to Rebalance Your Relationship* to strengthen positives and soften the charge of everyday irritants.

Harsh inner critic or self-doubt

Your default setting is to question yourself or brace for judgment. Even when things go well, you worry it's not enough, and the mental loop of "not good enough" becomes familiar background noise.
➔**See Remedy 5: Challenge the Tape** — *Rewrite the Narratives Holding You Back* to reframe old, unhelpful scripts.

Perfectionistic tendencies

Your mood rises and falls with how flawlessly you perform. Mistakes feel like failures, and the pressure squeezes out self-compassion and flexibility.
➔**See Remedy 6: Loosen the Grip** — *Build Emotional Agility, Not Just Control* to release the need to get it "just right."

Grieving a major loss

When grief reshapes your emotional landscape, finding steady ground feels harder than expected. Loss—whether through death, divorce, or life changes—alters the rhythms you once relied on.

➔**See Remedy 7: Tend the Wound** — *Let Grief Be a Teacher, Not Just a Burden* for support.

Overcommitted and emotionally depleted

If your calendar stays full but your emotional reserves stay empty, burnout isn't far behind. Giving generously without refilling yourself slowly erodes resilience.

➔**See Remedy 8: Recalibrate** — *Set Boundaries That Protect Your Capacity* to learn how to give without losing yourself.

Feeling unseen or under-appreciated

You keep showing up, but it feels like no one notices or values your efforts. Over time, that lack of acknowledgment breeds resentment and quiet fatigue.

➔**See Remedy 9: Reclaim Your Worth** — *Find Validation Beyond External Praise* to reconnect with intrinsic value.

Struggling to manage emotional input

When the emotional volume of the world—news, social media, group dynamics—feels overwhelming, your nervous system stays stuck on high alert. Recovery windows shrink, leaving you depleted.

➔**See Remedy 10: Filter the Noise** — *Protect Your Emotional Bandwidth* to tune back in to what truly matters.

Physical pain or chronic health issues

If your body is constantly demanding attention, it can quietly shape your emotional steadiness too. Mood, patience, and resilience bend under the weight of physical strain.

➔**See Remedy 11: Care for the Container** — *Support Your Body to Soothe the Mind* to address the body–mind connection compassionately.

Leaning too heavily on emotions to make decisions

When emotions rise, they can quietly drown out context, logic, or long-term vision. Without a steadier anchor, even heartfelt choices can sometimes drift away from what truly serves you.

➔**See Remedy 12: Balance the Scales** — *Honor Emotion, Anchor in Reason* to blend feeling with wisdom and create decisions that stand strong over time.

Remedies

🛠 This is your toolbox of practical steps to nurture calm, resilience, and joy. Pick remedies based on causes you identified in the previous section, or try any that spark curiosity. If one doesn't quite fit, try another—or mix and match until something feels right. Jot insights in your journal.

1 Find Your Triggers

Recognize Patterns That Hijack Calm

A dishwasher loaded "wrong." Someone cutting you off mid-sentence. Suddenly your reaction feels much bigger than the moment. That's because it usually is—it's the spark hitting old tinder beneath the surface. We all have emotional tripwires, and the goal isn't to never set them off. It's to catch them early, widen the pause, and choose a response you won't regret later.

Why This Matters

Unmanaged triggers can hijack calm in seconds, flooding the body with stress hormones that raise heart rate, blood pressure, and emotional reactivity *(American Psychological Association, 2019)*. Over time, this cycle wears down both relationships and health. Learning to spot triggers early restores choice in the moment and strengthens emotional resilience long-term.

☛ **Try This: When in Doubt, PaRC**

Your emotions leave breadcrumbs—if you learn to

notice them. This quick practice helps you map patterns and rehearse steadier responses.

Map the Pattern (5 min.)

Think back to 2–3 recent moments when your emotions spiked. Jot down what happened, how your body reacted (tight jaw, flushed face, clenched fists), the emotion you felt, and what you did next. Then ask: what was really going on underneath—feeling dismissed, embarrassed, exhausted?

Spot the Patterns (3 min.)

Now, review your responses. Do you notice any patterns—recurring emotions, specific people or situations, common times of day? Make note of them.

Practice PaRC (2 min.)

Choose one trigger from "Map the Pattern," above, and mentally rehearse a new response, using the PaRC method:

(Pa)use — Notice early body cues (racing heart, tense shoulders).

(R)eflect — Ask, *What's really going on here?*

(C)hoose — Select a response that reflects the version of yourself you want to show up as.

Write a short reminder—*When in doubt, PaRC*—and place it somewhere visible.

"Between stimulus and response, there is a space. In that space is our power to choose our response."
— Viktor Frankl

Reflect & Write

- What does that "space" between stimulus and response look like for you right now—how could you make it just a little wider?

Quick Tip

Your mind can't always tell the difference between imagination and reality. If you visualize calm responses often, your brain will remember how to choose them when it matters most.

For Further Exploration

Book: *Triggers: Creating Behavior That Lasts—Becoming the Person You Want to Be* by Marshall Goldsmith — A practical guide to spotting emotional patterns and reshaping responses.
Podcast: *The Happiness Lab* with Dr. Laurie Santos — Episodes on habit loops and emotional awareness offer science-backed insight.
Try It: Place a small reminder where you'll see it daily—on a mirror, your phone, even the fridge: *Notice. Pause. Reflect. Choose.*

Trail Marker: Your triggers don't define you. How you respond does.

2
Sit With It

Build Tolerance for Tough Emotions

Emotions can be messy and inconvenient, but avoiding them doesn't make them disappear. They resurface later—louder and harder to manage. Strength isn't about staying untouched; it's about learning to feel and still move forward.

Why This Matters

At first, sitting with a tough emotion may feel counterintuitive—as if you're rehearsing it, making it stick. The truth is the reverse: tracking that feeling gently can help calm your nervous system, much like pressing on a tense muscle makes it relax. Research shows that short mindfulness practices can lower anxiety, reduce emotional reactivity, and even shift neural activity in stress-related brain regions—proof that leaning in builds resilience, not adherence *(Psychiatry Research, 2024).*

☛ Try This: The 10-Minute Window

Think of this as emotional strength training—short, repeatable reps that make discomfort less overwhelming. The goal isn't to fix the feeling, but to prove to yourself you can stay with it.

Pick a Small Moment (2 min.)
Choose a recent situation that stung but didn't overwhelm you—like feeling brushed off in a conversation. Start with a ripple, not a tidal wave.
Notice Your Reflex (3 min.)
What's your usual escape hatch—cracking a joke, reaching for your phone, powering through? Naming your go-to move helps you spot it next time.
Sit and Stay (5 min.)
Set a timer and allow yourself to feel the emotion without distraction. Notice body cues (tight chest, restless hands, shallow breath) and ask: *If this feeling could talk, what would it want me to know?* When the timer ends, close the loop with a kind action—jot a note in your journal, talk with someone you trust, or step outside for air. Even three minutes counts as progress. Practice it on ordinary days, so it's easier to use on the hard ones.

"The emotion that can break your heart is sometimes the very one that heals it." —Nicholas Sparks

Reflect & Write

- When was the last time I let myself fully feel something uncomfortable instead of pushing it away?
- What did I learn from it?

Quick Tip

Discomfort is like a wave: it rises, crests, and falls. Ride it for a few minutes, and it usually loses its power.

For Further Exploration
Book: *Permission to Feel* by Marc Brackett — A compassionate guide to understanding, expressing, and managing emotions.
Podcast: *Therapy Chat* with Laura Reagan — Real talk on emotional awareness, trauma, and healing in everyday life.
Try It: Set a timer for 10 minutes this week and stay with one avoided emotion. Notice what shifts after the timer rings.

Trail Marker: The feelings you avoid don't vanish—they wait. Facing them turns them from intruders into teachers.

3

Press Pause

Use Micro-Breaks to Reset and Recenter

Stress has a way of hijacking the body—faster heartbeat, shallow breath, tunnel vision. It's not that you're broken; it's just your brain doing its overzealous "threat detected" routine (even if the threat is only an inbox full of emails). The trick isn't muscling through—it's learning to press pause, even for a minute, so your system can remember what calm feels like.

Why This Matters

Tiny pauses aren't indulgent—they're repair work. Just 60–90 seconds of stepping back can flip your nervous system from "go, go, go" to "reset and restore." Research shows that even brief breaks reduce stress, sharpen focus, and calm the body's stress response *(Occupational Health Science, 2021).*

"Almost everything will work again if you unplug it for a few minutes—including you."
— Anne Lamott

☛ **Try This: Build Your Micro-Break Menu**

Think of this like a pocket toolkit—low-effort resets you can use anytime, anywhere. The point isn't to stop the world; it's to rejoin it with a clearer head.

Stock Your Menu (3 min.)

Choose five quick resets that fit your life. It could be ten slow breaths, stepping outside for a moment, rinsing your hands in warm water, or humming a tune. Keep them simple and satisfying—like snacks for your nervous system.

Put It Where You'll See It (2 min.)

Write your list somewhere you can't ignore: as a lock screen, on a sticky note, or a reminder that pings when your day usually runs hot. Visibility is everything.

Practice Before You Need It (2 min.)

Try one break during a calm stretch of your day and

one when tension creeps in. Rehearsing in both states helps you grab the tool when it matters most.

Reflect & Write

- What are the first signs – in your body, mood or behavior – that stress is starting to build?
- What might make it easier to pause once you notice those signs?

Quick Tip

Pair a micro-break with a daily cue—standing up, logging off, or pouring water. The more automatic the hook, the steadier the pause.

For Further Exploration

Book: *Burnout: The Secret to Unlocking the Stress Cycle* — Emily & Amelia Nagoski's practical guide to completing the stress cycle.

Podcast: *The Happiness Lab* (episodes on rest and emotional agility) — bite-size science for everyday resilience.

Try It: Add a "Pause + Reset" reminder 2–3 times a day for one week. Each ping = one item from your Micro-Break Menu.

Trail Marker: A pause isn't an escape. It's a bridge—from reflex to choice.

4 Reset the Ratio

Use the 5:1 Rule to Rebalance Your Relationship

Retirement often brings more togetherness—fewer commutes, more shared mornings, and the creeping sense that your partner may be following you from room to room. That's when you begin to notice things. The sighing. The spoon clinking. The oddly loud way they open a drawer. These are the little sounds of love. Also: the little sounds of slow erosion to your sanity.

Why This Matters

It's not the blowups that wear a relationship down—it's the slow drip of unspoken irritations. Research shows that couples who thrive tend to offer five warm or affirming moments for every one moment of tension *(Journal of Family Psychology, 1999)*. That 5:1 ratio isn't a rule—it's a rhythm. A hum of goodwill that softens the sighs, the clinks, and the drawer slams.

"Successful long term relationships are created through small, frequent moments of turning toward." - John Gottman

☛ Try This: The 5:1 Reset

Think of this as emotional bookkeeping: for every debit of irritation, add five credits of appreciation. One of them must be spoken out loud.

Spot the Spark (1 min.)

Catch yourself in the moment when a partner's quirk grates on you. Chewing too loud, tapping a fork, the epic sigh—you'll know it when it arrives.

Stack the Balance (3 min.)

Right away, or as soon as you can, name five good things about them. Keep it small and specific: they fill the gas tank, make the coffee just right, text the kids encouragement, fold the towels, or still laugh at your corny jokes.

Say One Out Loud (2 min.)

Pick one of the five and share it directly. Bonus if it's unexpected: *"I know I grumble about the dishes, but I love that you always rinse the sink."* Little acknowledgments land big.

Reflect & Write

- What tends to fuel my irritation most – fatigue, unmet expectations, or something deeper?
- When my partner shows appreciation or kindness, how do I usually receive it – and could I let it land more fully?

Quick Tip

Keep a running 5:1 note in your phone. Each time you vent, add five appreciations from the same day.

For Further Exploration
Book: *The Seven Principles for Making Marriage Work* by John Gottman & Nan Silver — a classic on what keeps love strong.
Podcast: *Where Should We Begin?* with Esther Perel — candid conversations on evolving relationship dynamics.
Try It: For one week, practice the 5:1 ratio daily. At the end, notice how the atmosphere between you has shifted.

Trail Marker: It's not the quirks that undo a relationship—it's forgetting to balance them with kindness.

Rewrite Narratives Holding You Back

5
Challenge the Tape

We all carry old tapes in our heads—voices that whisper You're not enough, Don't mess this up, You'll never measure up. Sometimes they come from childhood, sometimes from culture, sometimes from a single careless comment that sank deeper than it should have. Over time, those messages can fade into the background—but they still shape how we see ourselves.

Why This Matters

Repeated thoughts form well-worn brain pathways—neural "trails" that grow stronger with practice. The good news? New trails can be built. Research shows that practicing self-compassion can rewire negative patterns, lowering anxiety and improving resilience *(Clinical Psychology Review, 2019).*

"Talk to yourself like you would to someone you love."
— Brené Brown

☛ Try This: From Critic to Coach
A journaling exercise can help you catch your inner critic in action and shift toward a kinder voice. Set aside 10–15 minutes for these three steps.
Name the Narrator (5 min.)
Your inner critic has a style—sharp, anxious, demanding. Whose voice does it echo? Give it a name or

persona—*The Perfectionist, The Old Boss, Mom at the Recital.* Naming creates distance and makes the voice easier to observe.

Decode the Script (5 min.)

Write down a thought that's been looping: "*I always screw this up.*" Ask yourself: *when does this usually show up? What emotion is underneath—fear, shame, inadequacy? Where might the script have come from? Would you ever say it to someone you love?*

Rewrite with Compassion (5 min.)

Take that same thought and answer it as if a friend, or younger you, had said it. Offer one gentle phrase that feels more honest and kind: "*It makes sense you feel that way, but it doesn't define you.*" Or "*You're allowed to make mistakes and still be worthy.*"

Reflect & Write

- Whose voice might be behind that narrative?
- What did I notice about how it felt to treat myself with compassion rather than with criticism?
- What truth about who I am became clearer when the critical voice softened, even briefly?

Quick Tip

Stick one compassionate phrase on a sticky note where you'll see it daily. Let it start replacing the old soundtrack.

For Further Exploration

Book: *Self-Compassion* by Kristin Neff — Research-backed practices for quieting the critic and cultivating kindness.

Podcast: *Unlocking Us* with Brené Brown — Brené and Kristin Neff on what self-compassion looks like in real life.

Try It: Write a short letter to yourself from the perspective of someone who loves you unconditionally. What would they say when you're being hard on yourself?

Trail Marker: Your old tapes may be loud, but they're not the whole story. You get to choose the voice that carries you forward.

Build Emotional Agility, Not Just Control

6
Loosen the Grip

Perfectionism wears a clever disguise. On the surface, it looks like drive and high standards; underneath, it's often just anxiety in a tailored blazer. When your sense of worth depends on flawless execution, it's not control—it's captivity.

Why This Matters

That drive to "get it exactly right" often masks quieter fears: *What if I fail? What if I disappoint? What if I look like I don't know what I'm doing?* Naming those fears shrinks their power. Research shows that examining worst-case scenarios reduces anxiety and builds confidence in navigating setbacks *(Behavior Research and Therapy, 2017)*. This isn't about loosening your grip entirely—just learning to flex, bend, and move without snapping

"We suffer more often in imagination than in reality."
— Seneca

☛ Try This: Fear-Setting for Perfectionists

Perfectionism thrives on vague, unexamined fears. This exercise brings those fears into the open and shows that even if the "worst" happened, you could recover—and that the cost of inaction may be higher than the risk of trying.

This exercise is adapted from author Tim Ferriss, who developed "fear-setting" as a tool for facing decisions that trigger avoidance. Originally designed for big life choices, it works just as well for shrinking everyday perfectionism—because unexamined fears lose much of their bite once named.

Define the Fear (5 min.)

Think of one area where perfectionism keeps you tense—a project, a routine, even a relationship dynamic. Write down the worst-case scenario if you showed up imperfectly. Be specific: *"If I submit this proposal with one typo, people will think I'm careless and never trust me again."*

Defuse the Fear (5 min.)

For each worst-case, ask: *How could I prevent this from happening? If it did happen, how could I repair it?* (Example: "If someone caught the typo, I'd correct it and thank them for noticing. My credibility wouldn't vanish—it might even improve because I handled it well.") Notice how the imagined catastrophe softens when you name your options.

Weigh the Cost of Inaction (5 min.)

Now flip the question: *If I keep clinging to perfection in this area, what will it cost me in 6 months? A year? Three years?* Write it down. Often, the price of inaction—burnout, resentment, missed opportunities—is far heavier than the price of an imperfect attempt.

Reflect & Write

- What am I most afraid will happen if I let go of perfect?
- What's one small area where I could safely experiment with "good enough"?
- How does the cost of inaction compare with the risk of trying?

Quick Tip

When perfectionism whispers "what if," answer back with "so what?" It's a fast way to shrink the imagined stakes.

For Further Exploration

Book: *The 4-Hour Workweek* by Tim Ferriss — Chapter on fear-setting, a practical antidote to analysis paralysis.

Podcast: *The Tim Ferriss Show* — Episodes where he unpacks fear-setting with entrepreneurs and creatives.

Try It: Choose one task this week to deliberately complete at 90%, not 100%. Notice what actually happens—and what doesn't.

Trail Marker: Perfection clings to "what if." Freedom begins with asking, "What's the worst that could really happen?"

7 Tend the Wound

Let Grief Be a Teacher, Not Just a Burden

Grief doesn't only follow death. It can arrive with divorce, a fading friendship, the end of a career, or the loss of an identity you once cherished. It doesn't keep a schedule, and it rarely asks permission. One moment you're fine, the next a smell or song undoes you. That's not weakness—it's proof that something once rooted deeply still matters.

Why This Matters

Grief is disorienting, but it also clarifies. Research shows that meaning-making during loss can strengthen resilience and deepen relationships *(Journal of Positive Psychology, 2017)*. The work isn't to "move on" but to move with—to carry the loss differently and with more kindness toward yourself.

"Grief is in two parts. The first is loss. The second is the remaking of life."
— Anne Roiphe

☛ Try This: Mapping the Terrain of Grief

Naming what's been lost and what remains can make the landscape less overwhelming. This reflection offers a simple map to help you walk beside your grief instead of against it.

Name the Loss (5 min.)

What or who have you lost? Go beyond a label—capture the texture of what's missing: *"Not just my job, but the sense of purpose I felt mentoring younger colleagues."*

Trace What's Changed, Anchor in What Remains (7 min.)

How does life feel different now—emotionally, physically, socially, spiritually? Has your sense of self shifted? Do routines feel heavier? Now, steady yourself by naming 3–5 people, practices, or places that still give you comfort and strength. Note why or how.

Give Your Grief a Voice (5–10 min.)

Write a short compassion statement:
"Right now, I'm learning to live with ____, and it's okay

that I feel ____."
If it feels right, extend it into a letter—to the person, role, or version of yourself you've lost. You don't need perfect words. The act of naming or sitting with the silence itself can be healing.

Reflect & Write

- What might I move toward, even as I carry this loss?
- What thread of meaning or steadiness could I tend now?

Quick Tip

Grief comes in waves. Instead of resisting them, practice surfing them—notice the rise, the crest, and the softening that follows.

For Further Exploration
Book: *The Wild Edge of Sorrow* by Francis Weller — A compassionate guide to grief as part of the human story.
Podcast: *All There Is* with Anderson Cooper — Honest conversations on loss, healing, and what remains.
Try It: Set aside one "grief day" this month—a walk, a journal entry, or a small ritual. It's not indulgent. It's human.

Trail Marker: Grief reshapes the map, but it also points to what matters most.

8
Recalibrate

Set Boundaries That Protect Your Capacity

Too often, we equate being available with being valuable. We say yes to things out of obligation, habit, guilt—or because we're not sure how to say no gracefully. But if your emotional tank is running on fumes, even the best intentions can sour into resentment, fatigue, or emotional detachment.

Why This Matters

When we overcommit, energy leaks into places that don't

align with our values. Research shows that strong boundary-setting habits can reduce stress and boost emotional well-being by up to 30% *(Journal of Occupational Health Psychology, 2018)*. Boundaries aren't selfish—they're what make generosity sustainable. For more on protecting your time and energy, see Remedy 4 in the Mental Well-being chapter. And if overcommitting shows up more as perfectionism than obligation, see Remedy 6 earlier in this chapter.

"Half of the troubles of this life can be traced to saying yes too quickly and not saying no soon enough."
— Josh Billings

☛ Try This: The "Hell Yeah or No" Filter

When everything feels like a "maybe," your time gets diluted. This filter helps you reclaim your best yeses and release the rest. This exercise adapts the "Hell Yeah or No" filter, a phrase coined by author Derek Sivers and often championed by Tim Ferriss, to make clearer choices with time and energy.

Scan and Sort (5 min.)

Write down 5–10 things you've recently said yes to—social invites, recurring obligations, even habits you keep out of inertia. Give each a gut-level rating:

- **Hell Yeah** — Energizing and aligned with what matters.
- **Maybe** — Lukewarm, habitual, or uncertain.
- **No** — Draining, stressful, or out of step with your values.

Get Curious (4 min.)

For each **Maybe** or **No** ask: *What keeps me tied to this—guilt, fear, habit? What would it feel like to let it go—relief or regret? Could I step back with honesty and kindness?*

Release One (3 min.)

Pick a **Maybe** or **No** and create a plan to decline, delegate, or renegotiate. Use a reframe: *"This no is really a yes—to protecting my energy so I can show up where it counts."*

Reflect & Write

- What might I reclaim by practicing a few strategic no's?
- How would it feel to save my best yes for what lights me up?

Quick Tip

Before saying yes, pause and ask: *"If this isn't a Hell Yeah, is it really mine to do?"*

For Further Exploration

Book: *Set Boundaries, Find Peace* by Nedra Glover Tawwab — Clear, compassionate guidance on identifying and communicating boundaries.

Podcast: *The Happiness Lab* — Episodes on emotional energy and burnout blend science with human stories.

Try It: Write a "reverse to-do list." Note three things draining your energy. Experiment with removing or outsourcing just one, and see what shifts.

Trail Marker: A no to what drains you is always a yes to what sustains you.

---

9 Reclaim Your Worth

Find Validation Beyond External Praise

There's nothing wrong with wanting to feel seen. A thank-you or a little applause can light you up—but if your well-being depends on other people clapping, you'll always be waiting for the encore. Retirement makes this especially tricky: the reviews stop, the kids don't need daily refereeing, and the question creeps in—Do I still matter if no one's handing out gold stars?

Why This Matters

Basing your worth on praise creates emotional whiplash—high when validation shows up, hollow when it doesn't. Research shows that people who ground their sense of worth in inner values feel steadier, more satisfied, and less anxious *(Journal of Personality, 2018)*. Reclaiming your worth means remembering that your value isn't up for negotiation.

☛ **Try This: Name What Matters**

When applause quiets, these steps help you shift attention inward and reconnect with your own grounded sense of value.

Spot Your Quiet Wins (5 min.)

Think back over the past week. List five small actions that mattered, even if no one noticed: listening well, making a hard choice, showing up when it was inconvenient, staying calm under stress, or tending to tasks others overlook.

Reconnect with Your Compass (4 min.)

Ask yourself: *What actions make me feel proud without recognition? When do I feel most aligned with the person I want to be? Jot down a few short reflections.*

Rewrite the Script (3 min.)

Complete this sentence: *"I used to believe I needed ________ to feel valued. Now I'm learning my worth shows up in ________."* This simple reframe begins to unhook your sense of value from others' approval.

"You alone are enough. You have nothing to prove to anybody."
— Maya Angelou

Reflect & Write

- Where have I already earned my own respect, but not claimed it?
- What daily actions remind me I matter—even when no one says so?

Quick Tip

At day's end, ask yourself: *"Where did I show up in a way I'm proud of?"* That one question shifts focus back to your own steady worth.

For Further Exploration

Book: *Radical Acceptance* by Tara Brach — A blend of psychology and mindfulness for reconnecting with intrinsic value.

Podcast: *Ten Percent Happier* with Dan Harris — Episode with Kristin Neff on self-compassion and inner resilience.

Try It: Spend five minutes a day writing down one way you showed up with integrity, kindness, or courage. Watch how the list grows.

Trail Marker: External applause fades. Self-respect endures.

10
Filter the Noise

Protect Your Emotional Bandwidth

Modern life runs loud. News cycles thrive on adrenaline, social media rewards outrage, and even a group text can morph from "just checking in" to "crisis in aisle five" in under thirty seconds. No wonder your system feels fried.

Why This Matters

Your emotional bandwidth is a limited resource. Constant exposure to negativity and high-stimulation input is linked to higher stress and lower well-being *(Journal of Applied Psychology, 2020)*. Protecting that bandwidth isn't about hiding under a rock—it's about choosing what deserves access to your head and heart.

"You don't have to attend every argument you're invited to."
— Unknown

☛ Try This: Build Your Emotional Filter

It's easy to forget that not everything deserves front-row access to your attention. This practice helps you notice what drains you, what sustains you, and set one small boundary this week to protect your peace.

List the Inputs (4 min.)

Jot down at least five things that regularly shape your emotional state—people, news sources, social media platforms, shows, podcasts, or recurring conversations. Name both obvious and subtle ones.

Check the Impact (4 min.)

Next to each input, note how it tends to leave you feeling: energized, drained, anxious, or mixed. Be honest—sometimes even "harmless scrolling" leaves a residue.

Try a Gentle Swap (3 min.)

Choose a single input to adjust this week. Will you eliminate (mute, unfollow, unsubscribe), limit (set a time cap, skip weekends), or engage differently (batch, skim, switch to print)? Finish the sentence: "This week, I'll adjust ______ so I can protect my energy for ______."

Reflect & Write

- What sources of noise have I mistaken for duty?
- What do I want to feel more of—and what needs to be filtered out to make space for it?

Quick Tip

Try a "low-input day" once a week—no news, no social media, no heavy conversations. Notice the space that opens up.

For Further Exploration

Book: *Stolen Focus* by Johann Hari — A sobering look at why attention slips and how to reclaim it.

Podcast: *The Calm Collective* with Cassandra Eldridge — Thoughtful, short reflections on boundaries and emotional balance.

Try It: Set a recurring "screen curfew" reminder on your phone. One hour before bed, step away from digital input and give your nervous system room to downshift.

Trail Marker: Silence isn't emptiness. It's space for what matters most.

11 Care for the Container

Support Your Body to Soothe the Mind

When the body hurts, everything else feels heavier—thoughts, moods, even patience with the people you love most. Chronic pain or fatigue doesn't just affect your body; it seeps into your routines, your confidence, even your sense of self. The good news? Emotional steadiness doesn't have to wait until your body "gets better."

Why This Matters

The body and mind are not separate. Pain and fatigue increase stress, while rest, movement, and comfort cues can ease the nervous system and restore emotional steadiness *(Journal of Behavioral Medicine, 2019)*. Caring for the container you live in is one of the most direct ways to care for your inner world.

"Caring for the body is not self-indulgence—it is self-preservation." — Audre Lorde

☛ Try This: Build Your Care Menu

On hard days, it's easy to forget what actually helps. This exercise gives you a ready-made menu of gentle actions you can turn to without overthinking.

Choose Your Options (6 min.)

Pick one small practice from each of these categories:

- **Movement**: Stretching, walking, tai chi, yoga, rolling shoulders
- **Comfort**: Heating pad, cozy socks, soft music, candlelight
- **Rest**: Sleep routine, screen limits, white noise, short naps
- **Nutrition**: Warm meals, hydrating drinks, anti-inflammatory snacks
- **Emotional Soothing**: Breathwork, journaling, guided meditation, a quick call with someone you trust

Write Them Down (2 min.)

Post your list somewhere you'll see it—bathroom mirror, fridge, journal—so on low days you don't have to think, just choose.

Adapt for the Day (2 min.)

Make two versions if it helps: one for "I'm just off" days and one for "I'm really struggling." Meeting yourself with compassion—not pressure—is the whole point.

Reflect & Write

- Where do I push through discomfort without asking what I need?
- What would it feel like to treat my body as an ally, not an obstacle?

Quick Tip

Even two minutes of body-kindness—a warm compress, a stretch, a glass of water—can signal safety to your nervous system.

For Further Exploration

Book: *The Body is Not an Apology* by Sonya Renee Taylor — A powerful exploration of radical self-care and honoring the body you live in.
Podcast: *Move Your DNA* with Katy Bowman — Insightful conversations about gentle movement and whole-body well-being.
Try It: Add a short ritual of physical kindness to your morning or evening routine. The point isn't to fix your body—it's to remind it of comfort and care.

Trail Marker: Your body is not the enemy. It's the companion carrying you forward—worthy of patience, kindness, and care.

12
Balance the Scales

Honor Emotion, Anchor in Reason

There's nothing wrong with being emotionally attuned—it's one of your strengths. But when feelings run the whole show, decisions that seem right in the moment can quickly unravel. The goal isn't to silence emotions but to give reason an equal seat at the table.

Why This Matters

Emotions offer important data, but without balance they can cloud judgment. Research shows that practicing cognitive distancing—stepping back to evaluate emotions—improves decision-making and reduces stress *(Journal of Applied Psychology, 2019).* Honoring the wisdom in your feelings while keeping your judgment clear creates a steadier foundation for choices that last.

"Educating the mind without educating the heart is no education at all."
— Aristotle

☛ **Try This: The Pause + Perspective Journal**
When emotions are loud and logic is quiet, journaling creates space for both voices. This reflection doesn't dismiss feelings—it simply balances them with perspective.
Name It (4 min.)
Write: *"Right now I feel..."* and complete the sentence

without editing or justifying. Naming the emotion loosens its grip.

Ask It (3 min.)

Write: *"This emotion is trying to protect me from..."* Emotions often point to something real, like safety, belonging, or competence.

Balance and Act (5 min.)

Write: *"What facts or perspectives might I be missing?"* Then choose one simple step that reflects this fuller picture—a call, a pause, a boundary, or even deciding to wait before acting. This anchors your reflection in movement, not rumination.

Reflect & Write

- Is this emotion offering clarity—or clouding it?
- If a friend shared this fear, what advice would I offer them?

Quick Tip

When emotions spike, say to yourself: "This is a feeling, not a fact." It's a gentle way to pause and invite reason back in.

For Further Exploration

Book: *Emotional Agility* by Susan David — A framework for acknowledging emotions while staying flexible.
Podcast: *The Tim Ferriss Show* — Episode on "Why You Should Define Your Fears Instead of Your Goals," for another angle on balancing emotion with perspective.
Try It: Run this three-step journaling practice on a small decision this week. Practicing in low-stakes moments builds the muscle for bigger ones.

Trail Marker: Feelings deserve a voice. Wisdom comes when reason gets one too.

Pocket Notes: Your Space to Reflect and Grow

Your Thrive Compass pointed you toward Emotional Well-Being, and now you have a clearer understanding of the emotional terrain you're traveling. Use the prompts below to deepen your self-awareness, notice small shifts, and plan practical steps forward.

Insights to Reflect On

- What stood out to me most in this chapter?
- Where do I feel strongest in handling my emotions right now?
- What emotions tend to overwhelm me—and when?
- What helps me manage tough emotions effectively?
- When do I feel most grounded or at peace?
- How do I define emotional well-being for myself?

Ideas to Explore

- Emotional regulation strategies I'm curious to explore
- Daily rituals that help stabilize my emotions
- Ways to show more self-compassion when I struggle
- Communication or boundary skills I'd like to grow
- Creative outlets that help me process emotions
- Old patterns I'm ready to observe with more curiosity

Actions to Take

- One emotional self-care habit I'll try this week
- A supportive person or resource I'll reach out to
- A grounding practice for when stress builds
- A boundary to protect my emotional energy
- One old story I'm ready to reframe
- How I'll celebrate emotional wins—big or small

Chapter Seven

Physical Vitality - Strength for the Long Haul

If your Thrive Compass pointed you here, your body might be whispering (or shouting) for a little extra care. Maybe your energy isn't what it used to be. Maybe a few aches RSVP'd without asking. Or maybe you've started wondering what it actually takes to keep doing the things you love—not just now, but twenty years from now.

This chapter isn't about chasing six-pack abs or pretending you suddenly adore burpees. It's about building the kind of strength and stamina that lets you carry the grandkids, dig in the garden, dance at a wedding, or just haul in the groceries without needing a nap afterward.

The Quick Start below will help you begin—at your own pace, on your own terms—toward a body that feels like an ally, not an obstacle.

QUICK START

How to Use This Chapter

📖 **Step 1: Start with "Mapping the Terrain."**
Get a feel for why physical well-being matters, and how it connects to your broader sense of balance and fulfillment.

👁 **Step 2: Explore "What Great Looks Like."**
Scan the statements in this section. Note when something resonates or sparks recognition.

🔔 **Step 3: Reflect on "Warning Signs."**
Move to the "Warning Signs" section. Scan and note any that feel familiar, even if it's just a small tug of recognition.

📍 **Step 4: Pinpoint "Possible Causes."**
In this section, gently explore the list. Notice any that resonate with your current experience.

🛠 **Step 5: Try "Remedies."**

Use the Possible Causes you reflected on as a guide. Turn to the corresponding Remedies to find practical, actionable steps you can take.

Throughout, use the Pocket Notes prompts at the end of the chapter—or your own journal—to reflect, capture insights, and shape any small next steps that feel meaningful to you.

🕮 Mapping the Terrain

Your body is the vessel that carries you through life—and in retirement, it deserves some attention. Not because it's "falling apart," but because you actually have the time to tune in. Physical well-being isn't simply about clean eating, spreadsheets or bootcamp workouts. It's about feeling strong enough to do what you love—whether that's a hike, a swim, or lifting a squirming toddler without seeing stars.

In this season, the rules change. You may not bounce back like you used to, or your joints might creak like old floorboards. That's not decline—it's just the soundtrack of being alive. The shift now is from pushing hard to sustaining long: strength, flexibility, energy, and resilience you can count on.

Think of physical well-being as your home base. When you're rested, fed, and moving in ways you actually enjoy, everything else steadies. Your mind clears. Your mood lifts. Your relationships feel easier. And most importantly, your confidence grows—because you trust your body to keep up with your life.

"My Own Journey" below shows how one small change in caring for my body rippled out far beyond the physical. From there, we'll explore what "great" looks like, how to spot the warning signs, and the small, steady shifts that let you age powerfully—and feel more alive in your own skin.

My own journey:

While visiting our daughter Kathryn in San Antonio, I spotted a tiny puzzle on her counter and thought, Why not? I sat down to tackle it, feeling pretty confident—until Jim and

Kathryn joined in and started solving three pieces for every one of mine. I kept smiling, but inside, I was thinking: Is this how it starts?

Cue internal panic. Was I losing my edge? Fortunately, I was knee-deep in my Retirement Transition Coaching certification and remembered a nugget of wisdom: sometimes, it's not your brain—it's your eyesight. Sure enough, after a quick trip to the eye doctor, I learned I needed a stronger prescription. New contacts, and voilà—I could see the tiniest details again, puzzle pieces and all.

It was a reminder that not all health slip-ups come with flashing lights. Skipping the eye doc or putting off that hearing test can snowball into much bigger things. When you're older, not updating your glasses doesn't just mean squinting at menus—it can mean stepping back from activities you love, like puzzling with your family or joining a book club lunch, simply because you're embarrassed or second-guessing your abilities. And that's where real decline can sneak in—not from age itself, but from quietly opting out.

Lesson learned: preventive care isn't about fear—it's about freedom. And yes, I finished that puzzle… eventually.

That's the thing about physical well-being—it's rarely about big, dramatic changes. More often, it's about noticing what's shifting, paying attention before small issues become barriers, and staying in the game—whatever your "game" happens to be. As you move through this chapter, take time to check in with what your body is telling you. Because thriving physically isn't about chasing youth—it's about respecting your body enough to help it carry you into what's next.

What Great Looks Like

Here's what physical well-being feels like when it's vibrant and strong. These qualities aren't about perfection but spotting what's already thriving or where a small step could add vitality. Write in your journal or notebook any that light you up.

- Moves with ease.
- Eats for energy.

- Sleeps like a dream.
- Stays mindful and calm.
- Keeps up with checkups.
- Bounces back fast.
- Feels good in your skin.
- Stays hydrated.
- Thrives with friends.

Notice what's already strong—and what small shifts might invite even greater energy, vitality, and ease.

🔔 Warning Signs

These are gentle creaks that your body might need a little TLC, like a boat needing a steady hand at the helm. They're not about fault—just a chance to tune in with care. Jot down in your journal or notebook any that feel familiar.

- Sits all day long.
- Feels lonely or disconnected.
- Craves junk food fixes.
- Sleeps the day away.
- Can't sleep enough.
- Feels tense non-stop.
- Shows signs of dehydration.
- Avoids check-ups or delays health screenings.
- Leans on drinks to chill.
- Eats past feeling full.
- Feels clumsy or slow.

These signs aren't about judgment—they're an invitation to reconnect with the strength, energy, and vitality that are still within your reach.

Possible Causes

Physical changes can slip in gradually, making them easy to miss. The table below helps name what may be affecting your energy, strength, or mobility by pairing common Causes with supportive Remedies. Note any Cause that resonates, then turn to the corresponding Remedy in the next section. Brief explanations below the table offer more context if needed.

Causes	Remedies
Lack of health know-how	1. Educate Yourself
Too many to-dos	2. Make a Plan
Stress overload	3. Take a Breather
Unhealthy surroundings	4. Build a Support Network
Tight budget	5. Be Resourceful
Lack of access	6. Bridge the Gap
Sticky bad habits	7. Spark Momentum
Feeling defeated	8. The Confidence Ladder
Skipping checkups	9. Stay Ahead
Ignoring body signals	10. Listen to Your body

Causes with Explanations

Lack of health know-how

Feeling unsure about what "eating well" or "getting enough movement" really means? With so much conflicting advice out there, it's easy to feel overwhelmed or discouraged before you even start.

➔**See Remedy 1: Educate Yourself** — *Cut Through the Noise and Get Clear on What Works* for a simple way to get back to the basics without the overload.

Too many to-dos

When life is full of to-do lists, appointments, and caregiving, your own health can slip to the bottom of the pile. Even if you know what you "should" do, finding the time and energy to actually do it can feel like a stretch.

➔**See Remedy 2: Make a Plan** — *Building a Routine That Works in Real Life* to set realistic habits that fit your actual day—not your ideal one.

Stress overload

Physical well-being doesn't exist in a vacuum. If your mind is constantly racing or you're feeling emotionally depleted, even small physical tasks can feel overwhelming.

➔**See Remedy 3: Take a Breather** — *How Rest and Move-*

ment Reset the Body and Mind for a gentle starting point that combines stress relief with body care.

Unhealthy surroundings

When your surroundings normalize poor habits—like junk food binges, substance use, or constant couch time—it's tough to stay vibrant. A social world that skips self-care or leaves you feeling isolated can quietly sap your energy, as loneliness weighs as heavily as unhealthy routines.

➔**See Remedy 4: Build a Support Network** — *Crafting Connections That Lift You Up* to create spaces that spark vitality.

Tight budget

If you feel like staying healthy requires an expensive gym, boutique supplements, or organic everything, here's the good news: it doesn't. Many of the best habits are free or low-cost.

➔**See Remedy 5: Be Resourceful** — *Healthy Doesn't Have to Mean Pricey* for practical ideas to work with what you have.

Lack of access

Whether you live far from a grocery store, have limited transportation to health appointments, or feel stuck without nearby parks or gyms, logistical barriers can make healthy habits harder to reach.

➔**See Remedy 6: Bridge the Gap** — *Creative Solutions When Wellness Feels Out of Reach* for ways to work around limitations and bring movement, nourishment, and care closer to home.

Sticky bad habits

Maybe you always skip breakfast, or the couch calls louder than your sneakers. Old habits can be surprisingly sticky, especially when they're tied to comfort or convenience.

➔**See Remedy 7: Spark Momentum** — *One Tiny Change at a Time* to break inertia and build new routines one simple step at a time.

Feeling defeated

Past efforts to get healthier may not have stuck, leaving you to wonder if it's even worth trying again. But change doesn't have to be dramatic to count—small wins build momentum.
➔**See Remedy 8: The Confidence Ladder** — *Rising Again After Setbacks* to rebuild confidence through small steps.

Skipping checkups

If it's been a while since your last checkup, it's easy to keep pushing it off. Yet regular screenings often catch small issues before they grow into big ones.
➔**See Remedy 9: Stay Ahead** — *Why Even Small Health Checks Make a Big Difference* to take that first step back into proactive care.

Ignoring body signals:

Pushing through aches or exhaustion might feel normal, but it drowns out what your body is trying to say. Tuning in doesn't require a huge overhaul—listening in small ways helps you catch imbalance early and recover more fully.
➔**See Remedy 10: Listen to Your Body** — *Small Steps to Hear Its Wisdom* for ways to reconnect with what your body is asking for.

Remedies

🛠 This section is your personal toolbox, filled with ideas to help you restore energy, build healthier rhythms, and feel more at home in your body. Pick remedies based on causes you identified in the previous section, or try any that spark your curiosity. If one doesn't fit, try another—or mix and match until you find what works for you. Share insights in your journal.

---

1 Educate Yourself

Cut Through the Noise and Get Clear on What Works

Health advice today can feel like trying to drink from a firehose—plant-based one week, fasting the next, and endless "experts" shouting over each other on social media. It's no wonder many of us throw up our hands and think, Forget it—I'll just do what I've always done.

Why This Matters

Conflicting advice breeds confusion and inertia. Research shows that people who feel confident in their health knowledge are more likely to make consistent, lasting changes *(Health Education Research, 2017).* You don't need a Ph.D.—just a clear filter that helps you focus on evidence-based principles and what fits your life.

"The greatest wealth is health."
— Virgil

☛ Try This: Your Wellness Filter

Before you chase the next "miracle" plan, pause. This filter helps you separate hype from help and tailor choices to what actually works for you.

Check the Source (3 min.)

Is this advice backed by solid research, endorsed by reputable institutions, and free from sales pitches? If it's mostly anecdotes or ads, skip it.

Check the Fit (3 min.)

Even good advice can be a bad fit. Ask: Does this make sense for my energy, budget, and lifestyle? Could I realistically keep it up next month?

Choose a Micro-Move (2 min.)

Clarity leads to action. Name one small step you'll take today—like a 20-minute walk, swapping soda for water, or scheduling your annual checkup.

Reflect & Write

- What health "rule" have I carried that might not serve me anymore?
- Where do I feel confident about my health choices, and where do I feel fuzzy?

Quick Tip

If advice sounds too good to be true, check whether it promises results "fast" or "for everyone." Real health never works that way.

For Further Exploration
Book: *Outlive* by Dr. Peter Attia — A research-rich look at the science of longevity, written with practical insight.
Podcast: *Ten Percent Happier* with Dan Harris — Evidence-based conversations on mindfulness and realistic change.
Try It: Pick one topic you're curious about—like mobility, protein, or sleep—and spend 20 minutes researching it using a trusted source (Mayo Clinic, NIH.gov, Cleveland Clinic).

Trail Marker: Knowledge is power only when it's yours—clear, trusted, and tailored to the life you want.

2
Make a Plan

Building a Routine That Works in Real Life

Life is sneaky. One minute you're promising yourself you'll walk more, eat better, sleep longer; the next, you realize it's been weeks and your "routine" is basically improvisation. That doesn't mean you're lazy—it means you're human. The fix isn't more willpower; it's a plan that works with your real life instead of against it.

Why This Matters

Routines reduce friction. Research shows that even one consistent health habit—like walking daily—can spill over and improve diet, sleep, and mood *(American Journal of Lifestyle Medicine, 2019)*. A plan that fits your actual days is more powerful than a perfect plan that never leaves the page.

"Discipline is choosing between what you want now and what you want most."
— Augusta F. Kantra

☛ **Try This: The Micro-Habit Blueprint**

You don't need a life overhaul—just one habit that slots naturally into your day. This blueprint keeps it doable, not aspirational.

Pick a Focus (2 min.)

Choose one area—movement, nutrition, sleep, stress, or hydration. Start where you feel the biggest pull.

Design the Habit (5 min.)

Fill in the blanks: *I will [specific action] at [time of day] on [days of the week].*

Examples: Take a 10-minute walk after lunch. Prep lunch before bed. Turn off screens by 9 PM

Smooth the Path (3 min.)

Set yourself up to succeed. Lay out shoes, prep food, or block time on your calendar—tiny cues make habits stick.

Reflect & Write

- What area of my health feels most ready for change?
- What derails me most often and how could I soften that roadblock?

Quick Tip

Track your micro-habit for seven days. Don't aim for perfect—just notice how often you show up.

For Further Exploration

Book: *Tiny Habits* by BJ Fogg — A practical guide to building habits by starting small.

Podcast: *Feel Better, Live More* with Dr. Rangan Chatterjee — Especially episodes on routines and burnout.

Try It: Pair your new habit with something you already do daily (e.g., stretch while coffee brews, drink water before checking email). Anchoring to an existing routine makes it stick.

Trail Marker: Small habits done consistently are what reshape a life—not grand gestures left unfinished.

3 Take a Breather

How Rest and Movement Reset the Body and Mind

When your body feels heavy and your mind even heavier, chances are you're running on empty. Stress and low moods don't just drain your emotions; they wear down your physical energy too. The fix isn't pushing harder—it's giving yourself permission to pause and reset.

Why This Matters

Movement and rest are powerful partners. Together they regulate your nervous system, lower cortisol, and restore a sense of calm *(Frontiers in Psychology, 2021)*. And the good news? You don't need a full routine—just small resets that help your body and mind remember how to recover.

"Sometimes the most productive thing you can do is relax."
— Mark Black

☛ Try This: Build Your 10-Minute Reset Ritual

Think of this as stress-prep, not stress-fix. By reflecting on when stress showed up recently, you can build a small menu of resets that will be ready next time you need them.

Recall Stressful Moments

Look back over the past week. When did you feel most stressed or depleted, and how did it show up in your body—tight jaw, foggy mind, low energy?

Pair Movement with Rest

For each situation, imagine one light movement (walk, stretch, one-song dance) and one short rest (sip tea, deep breathing, journaling) that could have helped.

Write Your Reset Menu

Create 2–3 pairings you can keep handy.
Example: When I feel tense, I'll stretch my shoulders and then step outside with tea. Use them as a ready-made toolkit for the next time stress hits.

Reflect & Write

- What does my body usually tell me when I'm stressed?
- Which pairing feels like my best "default" option?

Quick Tip

Keep one simple go-to reset—like "stretch + tea"—as your fallback. Simplicity makes it stick.

For Further Exploration
Book: *Burnout: The Secret to Unlocking the Stress Cycle* by Emily and Amelia Nagoski — A science-backed guide to completing the body's stress cycle through movement and rest.
Podcast: *The Daily Meditation Podcast* — Short, approachable guided sessions for anxiety, sleep, and resilience.
Try It: Pick one reset ritual from your menu and use it daily for a week. Notice if stress feels easier to navigate when your body and mind have a plan.

Trail Marker: Rest and movement aren't luxuries—they're the quickest way back to yourself.

4
Build a Support Network

Creating an Environment That Lifts You Up

It's hard to stay healthy when the world around you pulls the other way. Maybe your family teases your salad order, your friends treat happy hour like a competitive sport, or lonely evenings leave you drained. The truth? Your environment shapes your choices more than willpower ever could.

Why This Matters

Research shows that social connection is a key predictor of long-term health and longevity—sometimes more powerful than diet or exercise alone *(PLOS Medicine, 2010)*. When your surroundings reinforce your best intentions, healthy choices stop being uphill battles and start becoming second nature.

"You are the average of the five people you spend the most time with."
— Jim Rohn

☛ Try This: "What's In, What's Out"— A Connection Compass

This quick reflection helps you see which people, places, and routines lift you up—and which ones quietly pull you off course.

Scan Your Landscape

Think about your daily orbit—friends, family, text

threads, routines, online spaces. Sort them into three quick lists:

- *What's In*: supportive, aligned, energizing
- *Neutral*: neither helpful nor harmful (for now)
- *What's Out*: draining, misaligned, or subtly derailing

Shift the Balance

Pick one "In" to lean into this week—reach out, reconnect, or show up more. Then soften one "Out"—decline a plan, mute a thread, or step back.

Set a Reset Intention

Write it down: *This week I'll invest more in __________ and give myself space from __________, because my environment should reflect who I'm becoming.*

Reflect & Write

- Who genuinely cheers me on in my wellness journey?
- What parts of my daily environment already support the way I want to feel?

Quick Tip

It's easier to add support than subtract sabotage. Start with one uplifting person or space, and let the rest follow.

For Further Exploration

Book: *The Power of Habit* by Charles Duhigg — How cues and environments shape behavior, and how to rewire them.

Podcast: *Feel Better, Live More* with Dr. Rangan Chatterjee — Conversations on habits, identity change, and the role of community in health.

Try It: Make one micro-change this week—swap a sitting coffee date for a walking one, keep fruit in plain sight, or text a supportive friend.

Trail Marker: Sometimes the most powerful health choice isn't what you do—but who you do it with.

5
Be Resourceful

Healthy Doesn't Have to Mean Pricey

You don't need a $300 blender, a boutique gym, or a fridge full of superfoods to stay healthy. Some of the best wellness choices—walking, resting, cooking simple meals—cost almost nothing at all. The secret isn't spending more, it's getting creative with what you already have.

Why This Matters

Health advice often feels out of reach, but the basics are surprisingly affordable: Experts in lifestyle medicine point to six pillars—nutrition, movement, rest, stress management, relationships, and substance moderation—as drivers of well-being, not trends. Reframing wellness as creative and accessible—rather than costly or exclusive—makes it easier to build a healthy life with what's already within reach.

"Do what you can, with what you have, where you are."
— Theodore Roosevelt

☛ Try This: Your Low-Cost Wellness Menu

This reflection helps you uncover small, no-cost ways to support your body—simple habits you can start today without draining your wallet.

Pick a Focus Area

Choose one to start with: movement, nutrition, or recovery (rest and stress relief).

Brainstorm What's Free or Affordable

List 2–3 options in your chosen area. Examples: watching a YouTube stretch video, adding beans or frozen veggies to meals, nurturing a screen-free bedtime ritual.

Commit to One

Circle the one that feels easiest this week. At the end, ask: What worked? What felt energizing? What would I keep or tweak?

Reflect & Write

- What simple habit have I dismissed as "too small"?
- Who models healthy living on a budget—and what could I learn from them?

Quick Tip

Pair one habit with something you already do daily—like stretching during TV time or walking while you call a friend.

For Further Exploration

Book: *The Blue Zones Kitchen* by Dan Buettner — Recipes and stories from communities that thrive with simple, affordable habits.

Podcast: *Ten Percent Happier* — Episode: "Why Simpler Is Better," on how small shifts add up.

Try It: Challenge yourself to one week of zero-cost wellness habits. Journal what you notice about your energy, mood, or sleep.

Trail Marker: Wellness isn't about what you buy. It's about what you practice—consistently, simply, and within reach.

6
Bridge the Gap

Creative Solutions When Wellness Feels Out of Reach

You don't need perfect conditions to take care of your health—you just need a way forward. Maybe the gym's too far, the produce too pricey, or appointments are hard to reach. The goal is to find workarounds, not as consolation prizes but as real solutions that meet you where you are.

Why This Matters

Barriers like cost, time, and access keep many people from consistent wellness habits, but research shows that flexible problem-solving—finding "good enough" alternatives—helps build lasting health behaviors *(Journal of Behavioral Medicine, 2018).* Even small shifts, like swapping a long gym trip for a walk nearby, can keep you moving toward strength and resilience.

☛ Try This: Map Your Workaround

Wellness roadblocks don't mean stop—they mean detour. This exercise helps you name one barrier, then sketch a creative shift that keeps you moving forward

> *"Start where you are.
> Use what you have.
> Do what you can."*
> *— Arthur Ashe*

with less friction.

Spot the Sticking Point

Write down one barrier making health harder right now—maybe cost, transportation, energy, or scheduling. Get specific: not just "*exercise*," but *"I don't get to the gym because it's a 30-minute drive."*

Name Why It's Hard

In one or two sentences, explain what makes this a real challenge: "*It's difficult because* ______." This step turns vague frustration into something with which you can work.

Choose a Creative Shift

Brainstorm at least one workaround that makes this habit more doable—like trying a virtual version, breaking it into smaller steps, swapping timing, or asking for support. Then commit to testing it once this week. Afterward, jot down: Did it feel easier than expected? Did it remove even a little friction?

Reflect & Write

- What does my dedication to wellness reveal about me?
- What existing strengths or wisdom am I drawing on?

Quick Tip

The workaround you try doesn't have to be perfect—it just has to be possible.

For Further Exploration

Book: *Grow Wild* by Katy Bowman — Offers simple ideas for integrating more movement into everyday life, especially when formal exercise isn't an option.

Podcast: *Feel Better, Live More* by Dr. Rangan Chatterjee — Especially Episode #303, "The Power of Small Wins," which includes creative ways to boost health in everyday environments.

Try It: Pick one service or wellness habit that's felt out of reach and ask: *"What's the simplest way to bring this closer to my daily life?"*

Trail Marker: Health isn't about perfect conditions. It's about creative adjustments that keep you moving forward.

One Tiny Change at a Time

7
Spark Momentum

Big overhauls sound exciting but rarely last. What does? One small shift, so tiny it almost feels laughable, yet powerful enough to crack inertia. Start there, and before you know it, momentum takes over and the next step feels easier.

Why This Matters

Research on habit formation shows that small, consistent actions compound into lasting change over time *(European Journal of Social Psychology, 2010).* It's less about willpower and more about momentum—the power lies in showing up, not going big.

"The man who moves a mountain begins by carrying away small stones."
— Confucius

☛ Try This: One Tiny Change Tracker

When motivation is low, consistency beats intensity. This exercise helps you pick a single micro-habit and practice it for one week—long enough to prove to yourself that you can.

Choose Your Focus (2 min.)

Pick one area that feels off-track—movement, food, sleep, hydration, or recovery. Now name one action that takes less than five minutes (e.g., a short walk, adding a vegetable, filling a water bottle, writing down tomorrow's bedtime).

Define Your Tiny Habit (2 min.)

Name a single action that takes under five minutes. Write it as clearly as possible: *"After lunch, I'll stretch for two minutes,"* or *"Before bed, I'll sip water instead of scrolling."*

Track for One Week (3 min. daily)

Mark off each day you do it—on paper, in your phone, or with a sticky note on the fridge. Perfection isn't the goal; repetition is. At the end, ask: Did it feel doable most days? What got in the way? Do I repeat it, tweak it, or add another small stone to the pile?

Reflect & Write

- When during my day is it simplest to add it in?
- How do I celebrate progress without expecting perfection?

Quick Tip

Pair your tiny habit with something you already do—like brushing your teeth or making coffee. It's called habit-stacking, and it makes consistency easier.

For Further Exploration

Book: *Tiny Habits* by BJ Fogg — A practical, science-based guide to habits that stick by starting small.

Podcast: *Chasing Excellence* with Ben Bergeron — See the episode "Stacking Wins" for how micro-momentum builds confidence and identity.

Try It: Post your one small habit on a sticky note where you'll see it daily. Each checkmark is proof that change is already happening.

Trail Marker: Big transformations are overrated. Small steps, repeated with care, carry you further than you think.

---

8 The Confidence Ladder

Rising Again After Setbacks

When habits slip, it's not just your routine that suffers—it's your belief in yourself. After a few false starts, it's easy to feel stuck and wonder, Can I really do this? The way back isn't about doing more, faster; it's about proving to yourself, in small and undeniable ways, that you can keep a promise.

Why This Matters

Research shows that self-efficacy—your belief in your ability to succeed—is one of the strongest predictors of lasting change *(Health Psychology Review, 2011).* Starting small isn't just about the habit; it's about repairing trust in yourself, one win at a time.

> *"Success is the sum of small efforts, repeated day in and day out."*
> *— Robert Collier*

☛ **Try This: The Confidence Ladder**

Think of this as confidence training. Instead of aiming for the top all at once, you'll climb back one rung at a time, letting each success remind you: I can do this.

Name the Goal That Slips (2 min.)

Pick one area of health you've struggled with—like moving more, eating better, or getting consistent sleep. Write it down clearly.

Build Your Ladder (5 min.)

Now break that goal into five steps—starting with one that feels almost too easy to fail (that's the point.) Each step should get progressively more challenging. For example, if your goal is to move more during the day, the first step might be "Put on walking shoes each morning." The next steps could include: (2) walk to the mailbox and back; (3) walk around the block; (4) walk 10 minutes after lunch; and, finally, (5) walk 20 minutes three times this week.

Climb One Rung (variable timing)

Commit to just the first rung for one week. Don't skip ahead or "optimize." Let it become automatic. Then, decide: climb to the next rung, or steady yourself here a little longer.

Reflect & Write

- Where has my confidence taken a hit before?
- How do I feel when I keep even the tiniest promise to myself?

Quick Tip

Don't underestimate "too easy." The smaller the step, the stronger the foundation.

For Further Exploration

Book: *The Confidence Gap* by Russ Harris — A compassionate, practical guide to overcoming self-doubt and taking action.

Podcast: *The One You Feed (episode "How to Create Lasting Change")* — Realistic conversations on building confidence through small wins.
Try It: Pick one ladder rung and repeat it for 7 days straight. Notice how your confidence shifts—not in giant leaps, but in steady nudges.

Trail Marker: Confidence doesn't return all at once. It's rebuilt in small, steady steps—each one a quiet promise kept.

9
Stay Ahead

Why Even Small Health Checks Make a Big Difference

Let's be honest—nobody wakes up excited for a colonoscopy or hearing test. But preventive care isn't just about the big, scary stuff; it's also about the small tune-ups, like getting your glasses updated so you're not squinting at menus or catching hearing loss before it quietly shrinks your world. These little appointments act like guardrails, keeping you steady, connected, and ready for whatever's around the bend.

Why This Matters

Left unchecked, even minor health issues can chip away at quality of life. Poor vision, hearing, or oral health, for example, have been linked to social withdrawal and cognitive decline over time *(Journal of the American Geriatrics Society, 2018)*. Regular screenings keep the basics in check so your energy can go toward living, not worrying.

☛ **Try This: The Preventive Care Check-In**

Think of this as a wellness pit stop—an easy tune-up to see what's current, what's overdue, and where one small step might make a difference. You don't need to do it all at once—just spot what matters most and take one doable action.

Check Your Status (5 min.)

Jot down the basics—primary care, blood pressure, vision, hearing, dental, skin, mammogram/prostate, colonoscopy/FIT, bone density. Note the last time you did them and whether a next step is needed.

Spot the Hold-Up (3 min.)

If something's been lingering, what's the snag—cost, time, avoiding discomfort? Write down one small action to ease that block.

Choose One Next Step (2 min.)

Circle the easiest place to start. Make a call, ask for a referral, or set a reminder. Progress, not perfection, is the win.

"An ounce of prevention is worth a pound of cure."
— Benjamin Franklin

Quick Tip

Batch the admin: pick a 15-minute window once a month to schedule or confirm one appointment. Put it on the calendar like any other commitment.

Reflect & Write

- How might unaddressed basics (vision, hearing, dental) be shaping my daily life?
- What peace of mind would I gain from taking one small step this week?

For Further Exploration

Book: *Keep Sharp* by Dr. Sanjay Gupta — Practical guidance on protecting brain health, including the role of preventive care.

Podcast: *The Doctor's Farmacy (Mark Hyman)* — Episodes on prevention, root-cause care, and small steps that add up.

Try It: Within seven days, take one action—call a provider, request a referral, or set a screening reminder. Celebrate the step, not the outcome.

Trail Marker: Prevention isn't about fear—it's about freedom. Each small check keeps the road clear for the life you actually want to live.

10 Listen to Your Body

"Your body speaks; listen gently."
— Unknown

Small Steps to Hear Its Wisdom

In a fast-moving life, it's easy to treat the body as background noise—until it starts shouting. A sore back gets brushed off, fatigue becomes the norm, and tension gets filed under "just stress." But your body is always communicating. Those whispers of discomfort aren't nuisances to power through—they're signals pointing you back to balance.

Why This Matters

Mindfulness isn't just about calming the mind—it's about tuning into the body's early warning system. Research shows that brief check-ins with your physical state can reduce stress, improve self-regulation, and even lower inflammation *(Frontiers in Psychology, 2020).* Listening to the body doesn't mean fixing everything; it means responding with care before small signals grow loud.

☛ Try This: The Body Whisper Check-In

Think of this as a mini-conversation with yourself. You're not trying to solve everything—just pausing long enough to notice and respond.

Pause and Notice (2 min.)

Close your eyes, take a slow breath, and gently scan your body from head to toe. Write or say one phrase that captures what you sense: "My shoulders feel tight" or "I'm carrying fatigue."

Ask What's Needed (3 min.)

Without judgment, ask: What might this part of me be asking for? A stretch, water, stillness, or a quick walk? Jot one clear possibility.

Offer One Small Act (2 min.)

Do something tiny in response—sip water, roll your shoulders, breathe deeply. Then pause afterward to notice: Did anything shift? Even small relief is a sign your body feels heard.

Quick Tip

If scanning feels vague, use the "barometer" image: your body senses inner weather before your mind does. Tune in for a forecast, not a verdict.

Reflect & Write

- What signals have I been brushing off?
- What's one way I could respond with more kindness this week?
- How can I honor small cues before they become big problems?

For Further Exploration

Book: *The Body Keeps the Score* by Bessel van der Kolk — How body awareness fosters healing.

Podcast: *Move Your DNA* with Katy Bowman — Practical conversations about listening to your body's cues.

Try It: Do a 5-minute scan each day this week. Write down one signal and one response. See what patterns emerge.

Trail Marker: Your body isn't nagging—it's guiding. Every time you pause and respond, you reinforce trust in yourself.

Pocket Notes: Your Space to Reflect and Grow

Your Thrive Compass pointed you toward Physical Well-Being—and now you have a clearer view of the landscape your body is moving through. Pocket Notes are here to help you deepen your insights, notice small shifts, and map out sustainable next steps.

Insights to Reflect On

- What stood out to me most in this chapter?
- Where do I feel most physically alive and energized?
- What routines or habits have quietly drifted off course?
- What signals from my body might I be missing?
- Where do I tend to push too hard, or disengage entirely?
- How would I define "physical well-being" in my own words?

Ideas to Explore

- Small movement practices I'd like to build into my week
- Low-cost meals or snacks that nourish me and feel doable
- Creative ways to rest that feel refreshing—not just numbing
- Daily rhythms I can adjust to support better energy
- Physical activities I've been curious to try (no pressure)
- Assumptions about health or aging I'm ready to revisit

Actions to Take

- One 10-minute activity that supports physical well-being
- A processed food I'll swap this week for something healthier
- A boundary I'll protect for rest or movement
- A check-up I'm ready to schedule
- Something I'll do because it brings joy to my body or senses

Chapter Eight

Financial Confidence – Clarity, Control & Peace of Mind

If your Thrive Compass pointed you toward this chapter, chances are your finances are asking for a little more clarity or at least fewer late-night math marathons in your head. Maybe you're adjusting to a fixed income. Maybe you're wondering if you'll have "enough," whatever that means. Or maybe you just want to stop second-guessing every Amazon order like it's a life-altering decision.

Whatever brought you here, this chapter isn't just about budgets and spreadsheets (though we won't ignore them). It's about building the kind of financial confidence that lets you actually enjoy your life—without the constant undercurrent of guilt, fear, or "maybe I should've read that retirement article after all."

The Quick Start guide below will help you take your first step toward a little more freedom, a little less worry, and a clearer sense of what actually matters and what doesn't when it comes to your money.

QUICK START

How to Use This Chapter

🕮 **Step 1: Start with "Mapping the Terrain."**

Get a feel for why financial well-being matters and how it roots you in a thriving life.

👁 **Step 2: Explore "What Great Looks Like."**

Scan the statements in this section. Note when something resonates or sparks recognition.

🔔 **Step 3: Reflect on "Warning Signs."**

Move to the "Warning Signs" section. Scan and note any

that feel familiar, even if it's just a small tug of recognition.

🔍 **Step 4: Pinpoint "Possible Causes."**

In this section, gently explore the list. Notice any that resonate with your current financial experience.

🛠 **Step 5: Try "Remedies."**

Use the Possible Causes you reflected on as a guide. Turn to the corresponding Remedy to find practical, actionable steps you can take.

Throughout, use the Pocket Notes prompts at the end of the chapter—or your own journal—to reflect, capture insights, and shape any small next steps that feel meaningful to you.

📖 Mapping the Terrain

Financial well-being isn't just about dollars in the bank—it's about the story you tell yourself about money. In retirement, that story often changes: the paychecks stop, the nest egg becomes the lifeline, and the line between "enough" and "too much worry" gets blurry. Even those who look steady on the outside can wrestle with quiet stress inside.

This chapter isn't here to lecture or hand you a rigid savings plan. It's here to help you notice how money shapes your confidence, your choices, and even your joy. When you feel resourced—whether through savings, simplicity, or support—you walk lighter. You sleep better. You say "yes" to opportunities without the hum of fear in the background.

So what does financial well-being look like now? It might be learning to trust the shift from saving to spending. It might be creating rhythms that balance security with generosity or letting go of habits that keep you anxious long after they've served their purpose. Think of it as tending to a safety net, not so you can sit still in it, but so you can lean into the life you want to live.

And here's the ripple effect: financial steadiness rarely stays in its lane. It touches your stress levels, your relationships, even how free you feel to give your time and energy. In the next section, My Own Journey, I'll share what it was like to step into this new season with money—and the surprising emotions that came with it. Then we'll turn to practices and reflections that help you build confidence, clarity, and ease in your own relationship with money.

My own journey:

I wasn't prepared for how strange it would feel to stop saving.

For decades, it was second nature—socking away a little here, tightening the belt there, watching our retirement accounts (mostly) grow like a well-fed garden. I say mostly, because it wasn't always smooth sailing. There were dips that made our stomachs drop, market downturns that tested our resolve, and plenty of seasons where saving felt more like sacrifice than strategy. But through discipline and a lot of conversations around the kitchen table, we stuck with it.

And then... we arrived.

We retired. And suddenly, the accumulation phase was over. No more deposits. Just withdrawals.

It felt, quite honestly, like turning an hourglass upside down—the sand no longer rising, but slowly sifting away. Even though the numbers worked on paper (our financial planner had walked us through it many times), I found myself hesitating over purchases I would've never blinked at before. It wasn't about extravagance—it could be a new pair of running shoes or a weekend trip to see family—and still I'd feel that little twinge. Should I? Is this wise? What if...

Jim, ever the calm voice in the room, would gently remind me, "We did the work. This is what it was for." And he was right. But rewiring that saving mindset took time and trust. Not just in our plan, but in myself. That I wouldn't go off the rails. That we had, in fact, built enough.

The exercise in this chapter, Manage Your Money Mindset, wasn't just a worksheet. It was a mirror. Writing out my beliefs about money, then asking whether they still served me in this new season of life, helped me loosen my grip. It reminded me that spending can be an expression of joy, not recklessness. That being careful doesn't have to mean being afraid. And that peace with money isn't about never spending—it's about knowing what matters, and letting your resources support it.

👁 What Great Looks Like

Here's what financial well-being feels like when it's thriving—a safety net that gives you freedom to live fully. Scan these qualities, noting in your journal any that feel true or spark a quiet "yes." They're signposts of what's possible with small, intentional steps.

- Tracks money with ease.
- Adapts spending when circumstances change.
- Maintains a rainy-day fund for unexpected costs.
- Reviews investments and savings regularly.
- Manages debt wisely.
- Keeps insurance coverage up to date.
- Has strategy to reduce reliance on savings.
- Understands how taxes impact retirement income.
- Keeps estate planning documents current.
- Stays informed and financially curious.

Notice where financial clarity, flexibility, and security are already strong and where small shifts could bring even greater freedom, peace, and confidence.

🔔 Warning Signs

These gentle signals suggest your financial world might need a little attention, like a net with a few loose threads. Scan these qualities, jotting in your notebook any that feel familiar. They're invitations to strengthen your financial footing with care.

- Overspends often.
- Avoids budgeting.
- Skips check-ups on savings or emergency funds.
- Feels unsure about current insurance coverage.
- Carries stubborn debt.
- Doesn't feel confident about current investments.
- Ignores tax planning.
- Pushes estate planning to "someday".
- Withdraws from retirement accounts without a plan.
- Feels financially stuck or avoidant.

Noticing these patterns isn't about blame—it's about recognizing where clarity, attention, and small steps could start rebuilding confidence and ease.

Possible Causes

Financial unease can build gradually, making it easy to overlook. The table below helps name what may be affecting your sense of security by pairing common Causes with supportive Remedies. Note any Cause that resonates, then turn to the corresponding Remedy in the next section. Brief explanations below the table offer more context if needed.

Causes	Remedies
Lack of financial knowledge	1. Boost Financial IQ
No clear financial plan	2. Make a Map
Difficulty shifting from saving to spending	3. Manage Your Mindset
Spending or withdrawing too quickly	4. Pace Yourself
Underestimating how long you'll live	5. Design for Longevity
Facing unexpected health expenses	6. Build a Net
Financial stress from family obligations	7. Set Boundaries
Feeling social pressure to keep up	8. Spend Your Way
Navigating economic uncertainty	9. Future-Proof
Overwhelmed by financial decisions in retirement	10. Build Your Bench

Causes with Explanations

Lack of financial knowledge or engagement

If you feel lost in retirement rules, investment terms, financial planning, or home finance tasks—whether due to entrusting your partner with the details or not being "a de-

tail person"—you're not alone. Without a strong foundation or active involvement, it's easy to second-guess decisions or avoid making them altogether.
➔**See Remedy 1: Boost Financial IQ** — *Learn What You Need to Know* to build confidence with plainspoken, practical knowledge that fits your life.

No clear financial plan for retirement

When your financial future feels like a big, blurry question mark, even small money choices can feel shaky or uncertain. Without a guiding plan, it's hard to act with purpose or feel truly at ease.
➔**See Remedy 2: Make a Map** — *Create a Financial Plan That Guides You* to sketch a clear, flexible path toward your next chapter.

Difficulty shifting from saving to spending

Saving may have become second nature, but when it's time to enjoy what you've earned, guilt or hesitation creeps in. Instead of celebrating your hard work, you find yourself second-guessing whether it's okay to spend.
➔**See Remedy 3: Manage Your Mindset** — *Redefine Your Relationship with Spending* to ease into this new phase with peace and balance.

Spending or withdrawing too quickly

If your accounts are shrinking faster than expected, an undercurrent of worry can start to build. You may wonder whether today's lifestyle is nibbling away at tomorrow's security.
➔**See Remedy 4: Pace Yourself** — *Make Your Money Last* to find a rhythm that honors today's joys without sacrificing tomorrow's stability.

Underestimating how long you'll live

Focusing only on the next five or ten years can cause you to overlook the beautiful possibility of a longer life. Without stretching your timeline, you risk outliving the savings you worked so hard to build.

➔See Remedy 5: Design for Longevity — *Make Your Money Go the Distance* to extend your planning horizon and create more security later in life.

Facing unexpected health expenses

When illness or injury strikes, the financial impact often hits just as hard as the physical one. Without buffers, medical costs can quietly erode your financial footing over time.

➔See Remedy 6: Build a Net — *Protect Against the Unexpected* to prepare for life's surprises with more ease and less stress.

Financial stress from family obligations

You want to be generous, but helping loved ones financially sometimes stretches your budget past comfort. Over time, these sacrifices can build quiet resentment, anxiety, or strain.

➔See Remedy 7: Set Boundaries — *Give Without Losing Balance* to protect your relationships—and your own stability.

Feeling social pressure to keep up

When friends or family seem to be living larger—traveling, upgrading, gifting—it's easy to wonder if you should be doing more too. Comparison can subtly push spending beyond your true comfort zone.

➔See Remedy 8: Spend Your Way — *Align with Your Values* to adjust your spending choices with what you think is most important.

Navigating economic uncertainty

Rising costs, market dips, and policy changes can create background stress even when things seem okay day-to-day. Without flexibility built into your plan, uncertainty can feel overwhelming.

➔See Remedy 9: Future-Proof — *Build Flexibility into Your Plan* to create resilience that rides out ups and downs with less fear.

Overwhelmed by financial decisions in retirement

Navigating the many choices of retirement—such as

investments, budgeting, or asset management—can feel daunting and overwhelming. Uncertainty about making the right decisions can erode confidence and create stress.
➔**See Remedy 10: Build Your Bench** — *How to Choose Financial Support You Can Trust* to find wise, reliable allies for the road ahead.

Remedies

🛠 This toolbox offers practical steps to strengthen your financial safety net, from budgeting to planning for surprises. Pick remedies tied to the causes you noted, or try any that spark curiosity. Jot insights in your journal, letting small actions build lasting confidence.

1
Boost Financial IQ

Learn What Actually Applies to You

"Financial literacy" often feels like a class we somehow skipped. Even after years of working and saving, questions like Do I have enough? or Am I doing this right? can still feel foggy. The good news? You don't need a finance degree—you just need to focus on what actually fits your life.

Why This Matters

Uncertainty around money can quietly drain your peace, even when the numbers add up fine. Research shows that financial literacy and confidence—not wealth itself—are strongly linked to lower stress and greater life satisfaction *(Journal of Economic Psychology, 2019)*. Clarity doesn't mean knowing everything—it means knowing enough to move with confidence.

☛ **Try This: Build Your Personal Finance Playlist**

Money talk often feels overwhelming because it's everywhere and nowhere all at once—too much noise, not enough clarity. This practice helps you strip away the excess, name your resistance, and create a short, trusted "playlist" that fits you.

"An investment in knowledge pays the best interest."
— Benjamin Franklin

Name the Block (2 min.)
Write down the first reason that's kept you from digging in: *"It feels overwhelming," "I don't know who to trust," "I'll never understand it,"* or something else. Naming the barrier makes it less powerful.

Choose Your Style (3 min.)
Do you prefer to learn through books, podcasts, videos, or a friend explaining it over coffee? Pick the format that feels least intimidating.

Pick One and Test It (10 min.)
Find a single, plainspoken resource that matches your style and current need (budgeting, Medicare, investments, etc.). Spend 10 minutes with it—then jot down one insight or phrase that clicked. That's your first "track" on your financial playlist.

Reflect & Write

- What financial knowledge do I already possess without having named it?
- When have I made a money decision that served me well, and what does that reveal about my ability to understand what applies to me?

Quick Tip

Confidence grows faster when you learn in your own style. If you hate podcasts, skip them—pick the format you'll actually return to.

For Further Exploration
Book: *The Psychology of Money* by Morgan Housel — Why behavior matters more than spreadsheets.
Podcast: *HerMoney* with Jean Chatzky — Accessible, upbeat conversations about money and retirement.
Try It: Schedule one 15-minute "money learning" session this week. No mastery required—just one takeaway that boosts clarity.

Trail Marker: Financial well-being isn't about knowing everything. It's about knowing enough to move forward with confidence.

2
Make a Map

Create a Financial Plan That Guides You

When your financial future feels vague, even small choices—like taking a trip or upgrading the car—can spark doubt. Without a plan, it's easy to drift: spending here, saving there, but never knowing if it adds up. You don't need a complex system—you just need a simple map that lets your money serve the life you want.

Why This Matters

Studies show that even a basic financial plan can increase confidence and reduce stress in retirement *(Lusardi & Mitchell, 2014)*. The point isn't to master every number—it's to create a clear framework that reflects your values. When you do, decisions become less about guesswork and more about alignment.

"A budget is telling your money where to go instead of wondering where it went."
— John C. Maxwell

☛ Try This: Design Your Spending Map

It's not about spreadsheets—it's about clarity and confidence. This practice helps you align your money with what matters most.

Name Your Priorities (3 min.)

Write down your top three values or goals for this season—travel, family, security, generosity, or something else. If you've completed the "Visualizing Your Ideal Retired Life" exercise (Chapter 1) or Remedy 3 on Clarifying Your Values (Spiritual Well-Being), draw on those insights. If not, simply reflect on what matters most to you right now.

Sketch the Flows (5 min.)

List your monthly income and group expenses into fixed (mortgage, insurance, utilities) and flexible (groceries, hobbies, travel). Notice where the bulk of your money goes.

Spot and Adjust (5 min.)

Compare your spending with your priorities. Is there a mismatch? Circle one area to protect or grow, and one small shift you could make this week to bring things closer in line.

Reflect & Write

- How aligned is my spending with the life I want now, versus what others expect?
- What would simplifying my plan free me up to do?

Quick Tip

A plan doesn't need to be perfect, it just needs to be honest. Even one clear next step reduces the weight of uncertainty.

For Further Exploration

Book: *The One-Page Financial Plan* by Carl Richards—A refreshingly simple guide to mapping your money around what matters.

Podcast: *HerMoney* with Jean Chatzky — Practical conversations about money, values, and retirement realities.

Try It: Pick one spending category (like food or travel) and track it for two weeks. Notice surprises—and decide if it aligns with your priorities.

Trail Marker: Clarity doesn't come from controlling every dollar—it comes from letting your values lead the way.

Redefine Your Relationship with Spending

3 Manage Your Mindset

When you've spent 40+ years being praised for saving, it's no wonder that spending—especially on yourself—can feel...wrong. Even a modest splurge might trigger that little voice: "Is this responsible?" or "What if I need this money later?" But here's the thing, retirement is what you saved for, and it's time to give yourself permission to enjoy what you've worked so hard to build.

Why This Matters

Our relationship with finances runs deeper than numbers. It's shaped by decades of habits, upbringing, and the subtle rewards we've received for saving. Behavioral economists remind us that these internal "scripts" often drive decisions more than actual math *(Kahneman & Tversky, Journal of Economic Perspectives, 2013)*. Shifting them isn't about spending recklessly—it's about letting your values, not old fears, guide how you use what you've earned.

"The price of anything is the amount of life you exchange for it."
— Henry David Thoreau

☛ Try This: Rewrite Your Internal Spending Script

Old patterns don't fade on their own—they need to be surfaced and reshaped. This practice helps you notice the voices that hold you back and replace them with ones that give you permission to enjoy what you've worked for.

Step 1: Spot the Old Story (3 min.)

Notice a script that tends to surface when you spend—maybe guilt, fear, or second-guessing. For example: *"I don't really need this, I should skip it,"* or *"Spending on myself is selfish."*

Step 2: Reframe with Permission (4 min.)

Now rewrite that script into a phrase that feels truer and more supportive. For instance: *"I've planned for this, and it's okay to enjoy it,"* or *"This brings me joy, and joy matters too."*

Step 3: Practice in Real Life (5 min.)

This week, pause once before a purchase and test your new script out loud or in writing. Notice how it shifts the decision, the feeling behind it, or both.

Reflect & Write

- What message about money did I internalize growing up?
- In what ways do I treat spending like a failure instead of a choice?
- What would it feel like to use my resources in alignment with my values?

Quick Tip

Permission is powerful. A single phrase you trust can loosen decades of conditioning in the moment you need it most.

For Further Exploration

Book: *Die With Zero* by Bill Perkins — A fresh take on spending in retirement and using your money to maximize life experiences, not just your savings account.

Podcast: *The Retirement Answer Man* — Practical, mindset-forward tips on planning and spending wisely in retirement.

Try It: Create a short "joy budget"—a monthly amount designated just for things that bring delight. A class, a show, a great meal. Spend it on purpose and see how it feels.

Trail Marker: True wealth isn't just about what you keep—it's about how freely you allow it to support the life you've built.

Make Your Money Last

4
Pace Yourself

You've worked hard, saved faithfully, and now it's your time to enjoy it. But unlike a paycheck, retirement savings don't replenish every two weeks, which can make spending feel unsettling. The goal isn't to white-knuckle your way through retirement—it's to find a rhythm that balances today's joy with tomorrow's security.

Why This Matters

Research shows that people who adopt sustainable withdrawal strategies—like the 4% rule or dynamic spending adjustments—report higher confidence and lower financial anxiety in retirement *(Pfau, 2019)*. This remedy isn't about cutting back out of fear. It's about pacing yourself, so your money supports the long game while still funding the life you actually want.

☛ Try This: Take the Long View

This simple journaling activity invites you to zoom

"Nature does not hurry, yet everything is accomplished."
- Lao Tzu

out and examine your money through the lens of time. What's likely to change in 5 or 10 years? Are there surprises you're not budgeting for yet? By identifying big-picture needs, you can adjust without panic—and feel steadier today.

Name Your Horizon (5 min.)

Picture your life 10 years from now. Write down three things you hope you'll still be doing—traveling, hosting family, pursuing a hobby, or something else that matters to you.

Spot What's Coming (5 min.)

List 2–3 big events or expenses you expect in the next decade—maybe healthcare costs, home repairs, or milestone celebrations. Then add one "what if" scenario you can't fully predict, like inflation, caregiving, or medical surprises.

Choose a Tweak (5 min.)

Identify one small change you could make this month to stretch your resources without shrinking your joy—scaling back a low-value expense, slowing the pace of upgrades, or simply tracking one category to see where the money goes. Consider who might help you draw up a sustainable withdrawal strategy.

Reflect & Write

- Have I given myself permission to enjoy retirement while still protecting my future?
- What does "enough" look like to me—not just financially, but emotionally?

Quick Tip

Confidence often comes not from having all the answers, but from knowing you've built in room to adjust. Even one small tweak can create breathing space for the long haul.

For Further Exploration

Book: *Can I Retire?* by Michael Piper — A short, straight

forward guide to understanding retirement income and safe withdrawal strategies without overwhelm.
Podcast: *Retirement Answer Man* with Roger Whitney — Practical, approachable episodes for navigating retirement decisions.
Try It: Track one spending category for 30 days—not to restrict, but to notice patterns. Ask: What surprised me? What shift might bring more alignment with my values?

Trail Marker: Making your money last isn't about fear—it's about freedom. When you pace yourself with intention, you trade anxiety for confidence and create space for joy along the way.

5
Design for Longevity

Make Your Money Go the Distance

We tend to think in 5 or 10-year increments when it comes to money. But what if you live to 93—or 97? Planning for longevity isn't about penny-pinching—it's about giving your future-self options, so your long life feels supported, not restricted.

Why This Matters

Life expectancy has risen, but many people still plan as though they'll follow their parents' shorter lifespans. Research shows that financial confidence is higher among retirees who consider longer horizons when making decisions *(Society of Actuaries, 2020).* Widening the lens isn't about sacrificing joy today—it's about protecting your freedom tomorrow.

"Planning for tomorrow doesn't mean sacrificing today—it means giving yourself the gift of options."
— Inspired by Nancy Schlossberg

☛ Try This: Widen Your Horizon

This reflection stretches your thinking beyond the next 5–10 years, helping you imagine life at 90 and beyond. The goal isn't fear—it's clarity, so your later years feel steady and well supported.

Check Your Roots (5 min.)

Look at family longevity and health history. Ask:

What patterns—positive or challenging—might shape my own future?

Picture 95 (5 min.)

Imagine your life at 95. Would your current financial habits allow you to live in the way you hope—active, comfortable, and connected?

Spot Big Costs (5 min.)

Consider later-life expenses like caregiving, housing transitions, or mobility tools. Write down one financial move today—like building a care fund or exploring long-term care options—that could lighten tomorrow's load.

Reflect & Write

- How do I want my later years to feel—liberated, limited, or somewhere in between?
- What financial decisions today can give me peace of mind tomorrow?
- Am I planning based on outdated assumptions, or on what's possible?

Quick Tip

Try an online life expectancy calculator (like Blue Zones or SSA.gov). It can shift how you view your timeline—and spark fresh priorities.

For Further Exploration

Book: *How to Make Your Money Last* by Jane Bryant Quinn — A practical guide to stretching retirement income across decades.

Podcast: *The New Retirement Podcast* — Expert conversations on longevity, financial planning, and designing your later years

Try It: Use a simple life expectancy calculator and ask: If this number is right, what would I want to adjust in my financial plan today?

Trail Marker: Longevity planning isn't about fear—it's about freedom. The longer the horizon you plan for, the more confidence you'll carry into every year.

Protect Against the Unexpected

6
Build a Net

Health surprises have a way of showing up uninvited—and they rarely send a heads-up. Even with good insurance, gaps and deductibles can pile on fast, creating financial stress right when you least need it. A safety net isn't about bracing for disaster—it's about building resilience, so you feel steadier no matter what comes.

Why This Matters

Medical expenses remain one of the top financial concerns in retirement, with out-of-pocket costs averaging over $300,000 for a couple across their lifetime *(Fidelity, 2023).* Planning ahead with buffers, flexible coverage, and contingency strategies can reduce stress and give you more control. Shifting "what if" from panic to preparation creates a steadier sense of peace and confidence.

"Preparation is not about predicting the future—it's about strengthening your ability to face it."
— Adapted from Atul Gawande

☛ Try This: Map Your Safety Net

Health costs can sneak up quietly, but a little foresight goes a long way. This practice helps you anticipate possible curveballs and sketch out how you'd meet them without panic.

Scan the Timeline (5 min.)

Divide your page into short-term (1–2 years), mid-term (3–10 years), and long-term (10+ years). For each, jot down possible health expenses—like dental implants, joint surgery, or caregiving support.

Spot the Gaps (5 min.)

Ask yourself: Do I already have a plan for these costs? If not, what would help—savings, an HSA, insurance review, or a dedicated buffer? This is contingency planning, not catastrophe planning.

Choose One Step (5 min.)

Pick a single action to take this month—reviewing last year's medical spending, adjusting coverage, or earmarking a small savings cushion. Focus on progress, not perfection.

Reflect & Write

- What health-related expenses have caught me off guard in the past?
- Do I have the right support (insurance, savings, knowledge) to feel prepared for the next big surprise?

Quick Tip

Even a modest buffer makes a big difference. Think of it as building emotional as well as financial resilience.

For Further Exploration
Book: *Being Mortal* by Atul Gawande — A compassionate look at aging, medical decision-making, and quality of life.
Podcast: *HerMoney* with Jean Chatzky – Episode: "Health Care Costs in Retirement."
Try It: Review your last 12 months of health-related spending. What portion was expected vs. unexpected? Use this as a baseline for your emergency health buffer.

Trail Marker: A safety net isn't just money set aside—it's peace of mind woven into your future.

7
Set Boundaries

Give Without Losing Balance

Helping family often feels like the right thing to do and many times, it is. But when help starts to chip away at your own stability, generosity can quietly slip into obligation. Boundaries aren't about saying "no" to love; they're about protecting both your peace of mind and your future self.

Why This Matters

Research shows that financial strain from supporting family can erode retirement confidence and even increase anxiety and resentment *(Pew, 2019)*. Healthy boundaries ensure that generosity remains joyful, not depleting. Aligning your giving with your values—not just your reflexes—helps you stay grounded in both care and clarity.

> *"Generosity is not measured by how much you give away, but by how freely you give within your limits."*
> *— Inspired by Brené Brown*

☛ Try This: Clarify Your Comfort Zone

When giving becomes automatic, it's time to pause. This reflection helps you spot where generosity and guilt might be tangled—and sketch boundaries that feel both loving and sustainable.

Review Recent Requests (5 min.)

In your journal, make a note of the last few times you were asked for financial help—big or small. Jot down what you said and how you felt afterward (proud, strained, obligated, relieved).

Spot the Signal (5 min.)

Notice mismatches between your emotions and your actions. Did you say "yes" but feel tense? Or "no" but with lingering guilt? Was it an expense you could even afford? These are cues that a clearer boundary may be needed.

Draw Your Healthy Line (5 min.)

Write one simple boundary statement for each, such as "I'll only give if it doesn't dip into savings" or "I'll help with joyful gifts, not ongoing expenses." Keep it visible as a reminder when the next request comes.

Reflect & Write

- What does generosity look like when it includes my well-being?
- What kind of support can I give that aligns with both love and limits?

Quick Tip

A clear boundary doesn't close the door on love—it keeps generosity from turning into quiet resentment.

For Further Exploration
Book: *Set Boundaries, Find Peace* by Nedra Glover Tawwab — A compassionate guide to practicing healthy limits in every area of life, including finances.
Podcast: *The Dave Ramsey Show* – Episode: "Family and Finances."
Try It: Revisit one recent financial request using your new boundary statement. Notice how it feels to respond with clarity instead of reflex.

Trail Marker: True generosity doesn't drain you—it sustains you and the people you care about.

8
Spend Your Way

Align with Your Values

Retirement can bring a subtle pressure—not to earn more, but to show more. Keeping up with friends' remodels, trips, or gifts to grandkids can make you wonder if you're doing enough, even when no one's keeping score. The truth is that the most meaningful spending choices are the ones that reflect your values—not anyone else's.

Why This Matters

Research shows that values-based spending increases life satisfaction and reduces regret, even when total spending is modest *(Howell et al., 2013).* When your money choices reflect what matters most to you, they carry less stress and more meaning. Filtering out the noise lets your financial decisions support joy, peace, and purpose.

"Too many people spend money they haven't earned, to buy things they don't want, to impress people they don't like."
— Will Rogers

☛ Try This: The "Worth It" Filter
Comparison-driven spending decisions rarely bring lasting joy. This practice helps you pause, reflect, and reset so your choices feel rooted in your values—not outside pressure.
Spot the Pressure (3 min.)
Note a spending situation that's creating pressure or

uncertainty right now—maybe a purchase, trip, or gift. Write down what's triggering it and where the pressure is coming from—friends, ads, family, or even your own expectations.

Ask the Filter Questions (5 min.)

Ask yourself: *Am I genuinely excited about this, or just afraid of missing out?* If I say yes to it, what do I give up? If I say no, what really happens? Write your answers honestly.

Reconnect with Your Vision (5 min.)

If you've done the "Visualizing Your Ideal Retired Life" exercise (Chapter 1) or Remedy 3 on Clarifying Your Values (Spiritual Well-Being), use those insights as your guide. If not, simply list 2–3 qualities that matter most to you right now—like freedom, generosity, or peace—and filter your decision through them. Decide: Does this choice move me any closer to what's most important? Note your next step with clarity.

Reflect & Write

- What purchases or experiences in the past year felt truly worth it?
- Where have I felt pressure to say yes, even when it didn't align with my values?

Quick Tip

Alignment beats approval. Spending in line with your values is the real measure of financial success.

For Further Exploration

Book: *Your Money or Your Life* by Vicki Robin — A thoughtful guide to aligning spending with purpose.

Podcast: *The Minimalists Podcast* — Conversations on decluttering finances and life.

Try It: For one week, pause before every non-essential purchase. Ask: "Is this for me—or for someone else's approval?" Journal what you discover.

Trail Marker: Money well spent isn't about more—it's about meaning.

9

Future Proof

Build Flexibility Into Your Plan

Uncertainty isn't just something that happens on Wall Street anymore—it shows up in grocery aisles, insurance premiums, and portfolio balances. That can feel unsettling when your retirement income is more fixed than flexible. But adaptability isn't luck—it's a skill you can practice, and it starts with giving your plan a little built-in give.

Why This Matters

Research shows that households with flexible withdrawal and spending strategies report lower stress and greater retirement satisfaction, even during downturns *(Pfau, 2019).* Financial resilience isn't about expecting the worst—it's about knowing you have room to bend without breaking. A flexible plan helps you feel grounded today while staying prepared for tomorrow.

"It's not the strongest that survive, but those most adaptable to change."
— Charles Darwin

☛ Try This: Stress-Test Your Plan

Think of this as a rehearsal for financial curveballs. By walking through a few "what ifs," you'll see where your plan feels steady—and where a little flexibility could add peace of mind.

Choose Your Scenarios (5 min.)

Look at the list below and circle 2–3 that feel most realistic or concerning for you. These will be the "test cases" you'll use to stress-test your plan:

- Inflation increases everyday expenses by 10%
- Your investment portfolio drops 15%
- Health insurance premiums rise unexpectedly
- A home repair, car issue, or roof replacement is suddenly needed
- A family member asks for financial help

Run the Dry Run (10 min.)

For each scenario, ask: *How would this affect my life*

style, budget, or sense of calm? Would my current income, savings, or insurance set-up absorb it—or strain under it?

Sketch a Soft Pivot (5 min.)

Brainstorm 1-2 proactive adjustments for each case—building a buffer fund, trimming one expense, rebalancing with an advisor, or planning big-ticket costs ahead.

Reflect & Write

- Am I leaning too heavily on everything going perfectly as planned?
- What's one small step I could take this month to feel more financially agile?

Quick Tip

If your go-to answer is always "dip into savings," that's a nudge to strengthen your safety net—through cash buffers, insurance, or diversification.

For Further Exploration

Book: *How to Make Your Money Last* by Jane Bryant Quinn — Practical guidance on building income that adjusts as life unfolds.

Podcast: *The New Retirement Podcast – "How to Plan for the Unexpected"* — Experts discuss emotional and financial readiness for change.

Try It: Take one "what if" from the exercise and map out your response. Knowing the next step ahead of time reduces fear and builds resilience.

Trail Marker: Flexibility is freedom. When your plan has room to bend, you don't just survive surprises—you move through them with confidence.

10 Build Your Bench

How to Choose Financial Support You Can Trust

Money can feel complicated, emotional, and sometimes overwhelming—especially in retirement when you're shifting from saving to spending. Even the most careful planner can feel uneasy about whether they're making the right calls. The good news? You don't have to go it alone—you just need the right kind of support.

Why This Matters

Research shows that working with a trusted, fiduciary financial advisor can increase retirement confidence and reduce stress around money decisions *(Collins, 2021)*. But the key is knowing what to look for: clarity, transparency, and a relationship that aligns with your needs and values. Choosing a financial partner isn't just a money move—it's a trust move. And like any important relationship, it should be based on clarity, shared values, and mutual respect.

"A good financial advisor is a teacher, not a salesperson." — *Suze Orman*

☛ Try This: Clarify and Ask with Confidence

Finding a financial advisor shouldn't feel like cracking a secret code. This practice helps you get clear on what you need, and what to ask, so the conversation feels empowering—not intimidating. Write your answers to the following and share them with someone you trust.

Clarify Your Needs (5 min.)

List the areas you'd most like help with—withdrawals, taxes, investments, Medicare, estate planning, or simply peace of mind. Note whether you prefer ongoing guidance, a one-time consultation, or an as-needed check-in.

Ask About Costs (5 min.)

Prepare 2–3 essential questions: Are you a fiduciary 100% of the time? How are you compensated? What are your total fees? Compensation models vary. What matters most is transparency. Ask for costs in real dollar terms so you know exactly what you're paying for the value you receive. Even small percentages can quietly add up: a 1% fee on a $700,000 portfolio equals $7,000 a year!

Spot Your Fit (5 min.)

Ask about their philosophy, the tools they use, and

how they tailor advice to your goals. After the conversation, reflect: Did you feel heard? Did the answers build trust or raise red flags? You're not just hiring expertise—you're building a relationship grounded in clarity and trust.

Reflect & Write

- What would a trusted financial partner free me up to focus on?
- Where do I feel most confident handling money—and where could I use a second set of eyes?

Quick Tip

You don't need to hire the first advisor you meet. Interview at least two so you can compare approaches, personalities, and transparency side by side.

For Further Exploration

Book: *The New Retirementality* by Mitch Anthony — A smart, engaging read on how retirement has changed and what that means for financial planning.

Website: *www.napfa.org* — Search for fee-only fiduciary advisors near you.

Try It: Ask a financially confident friend how they chose their advisor. Sometimes, lived experience is the best referral guide.

Trail Marker: The right advisor isn't someone who dazzles you with jargon—they're someone who helps you feel steady, informed, and free to live the life you've planned.

Pocket Notes: Your Space to Reflect and Grow

Your Thrive Compass pointed to Financial Confidence—now capture what's emerging. Use your journal to sketch insights, goals, or steps for a clearer financial life. No rules, just what feels true.

Insights to Reflect On

- What stood out to me most in this chapter?
- How do I currently feel about my money habits?
- What brings me the most financial peace?
- How do finances shape my overall well-being?
- Which beliefs about money might need redefining?
- How would I define "financial confidence"?

Ideas to Explore

- Specific financial habits I'd like to strengthen or adjust
- Practical ways I could simplify or streamline my spending
- Trusted sources for financial guidance or support
- New investing perspectives I'm curious to explore
- Financial topics or skills I'd like to learn
- Core values I want reflected in financial decisions

Actions to Take

- One small spending habit I'm ready to change or improve
- A step I'll take to clarify or strengthen my emergency fund
- Schedule time to review plans with an advisor
- Update my estate or legacy planning checklist
- Revisit my retirement strategy with new eyes
- A money task I've avoided, but now feel ready for

Chapter Nine

Thriving is a Practice, Not a Destination

Congratulations! By picking up this guide—and more importantly, by engaging with it—you've already done something powerful: you've chosen to be intentional about your life after retirement.

That's no small thing.

In a world that often dwells on what's left behind when we stop working, you've focused on what you're moving toward: clarity, connection, purpose, and joy. That choice—to reflect, to reassess, to stay curious—is the essence of thriving.

And here's the truth: thriving isn't a finish line you cross. It's a practice you return to, again and again, through every new season of life.

Seasons Will Shift—and So Will You

There will be times when your physical vitality feels strong and steady, but your social world feels thinner—like different seasons along a path. Other times, emotional steadiness may anchor you, even if financial uncertainty rattles the edges. Some chapters will brim with purpose and flow; others may feel more like wandering in the fog.

This is normal.

Thriving doesn't mean mastering all six pathways of the Thrive Compass—Spiritual Meaning, Mental Clarity, Social Connection, Emotional Balance, Physical Vitality, and Financial Confidence—at once. It means noticing where you are, responding with kindness, and trusting you have the tools to adjust.

Your Thrive Compass: A Living Guide

As you move through retirement (and through life) your

needs, desires, and challenges will evolve. That's exactly why this guide was designed: to meet you wherever you are.

The Thrive Compass isn't something you complete and set aside. It's a reference point you can return to anytime you feel off-track, uncertain, or simply curious about where you are now. Not to judge or fix, but to notice. To gently reorient. To remind yourself of what's already working.

You don't need to revisit everything at once. Often, clarity comes from paying attention to just one pathway of thriving at a time—especially the one that feels most alive, or most tender, in this season.

A simple self-check can help you reconnect with yourself and your direction:

- Where do I feel strongest right now?
- Where do I feel stretched or tender?

That's enough.

You don't need a massive overhaul. Small, steady adjustments—the kind you've practiced throughout this guide—create lasting change.

Thriving, after all, is built one mindful step at a time.

Final Reflection: Your Story Is Still Being Written

Retirement isn't the end of your story—it's a new chapter, full of possibility. Like Jim, you might fill it with bold new roles. Like me, you might explore slowly, seeking clarity before action. Both paths are valid, and both are yours to shape.

There will be blank pages, and there will be unexpected plot twists. Some days will feel rich with momentum; others will feel quiet and slow. Both are part of the tapestry.

The key is this:

Stay awake to your own life.

Stay curious.
Stay kind—to yourself and your journey.

"We do not grow absolutely, chronologically. We grow sometimes in one dimension, and not in another; unevenly."
—Anaïs Nin

Thriving isn't about being perfect. It's about showing up—with clarity, with heart, and with a willingness to evolve. You're already on the path.

Keep going.

Trail Marker: Thriving isn't a destination on the map—it's the way you walk the path. You began this journey wondering where the map might lead; now you hold a compass that will guide you through every new season. With each step, you're already shaping a life that is wholly, beautifully yours.

Bonus Tool

Thrive Compass Victory Board

Before you set this guide aside, here's one last practice to keep your momentum alive.

By now, you've taken a powerful journey through your Thrive Compass—reflecting, assessing, and experimenting with new ways to flourish. This tool gives you a simple way to mark that journey, celebrate progress, and gently steer toward what's next.

Thriving isn't about big leaps—it's about noticing the small wins and staying connected to what matters most. The Victory Board is a simple, flexible space—paper, sticky notes, or even a mental snapshot—where you can pin your progress and point yourself toward what's next.

Think of it as a living reminder: You're not drifting through retirement—you're steering with intention.

And here's the key: this tool ties back to the vision you crafted early in the book: your Life That's Most You and your Ideal Retired Day. By linking your wins and next steps to that foundation, you reinforce your journey with authenticity and purpose.

☛ **Try This: Mark Your Wins, Map Your Next Step**

Every few months (quarterly works well—or anytime you need a lift), take just 5–10 minutes and check in. Grab your journal or use the Pocket Notes in this guide.

Pick Your Focus (2 min.)

Think back to the Thrive Assessment. Choose one of the six pathways you've been working on recently:

- Spiritual Meaning
- Mental Clarity

The journey is the reward."
— Taoist proverb

- Social Connection
- Emotional Balance
- Physical Vitality
- Financial Confidence

Make that dimension the center of this check-in.

Celebrate a Win (3 min.)

What's one small victory from the past season that reflects your ideal self or retirement vision? For example: "Joined a hiking group, like my vision of morning walks" (Physical).

Picture What's Next (5 min.)

Now imagine one vivid step that would deepen this dimension, inspired by your Chapter 1 insights. For example: "Sharing coffee with a new friend, like my vision of cozy chats" (Social).

Victory Board Notes

- Dimension: ______________________
- Win: ___________________________
- Next Step Image: _________________

Trail Marker: This tool isn't about piling on more goals—it's about savoring what's already unfolding and keeping your vision alive. By tying your wins and dreams to the self you uncovered early on, you create a rhythm of growth that feels natural and true. A few quick check-ins each year, and your Victory Board will quietly remind you: you're thriving already.

Acknowledgements

No guide is ever truly written alone.

I am deeply grateful to Jim, whose steady encouragement and grounded wisdom have been a compass of their own throughout this project—and throughout life.

My heartfelt thanks to Jackie Hamel—my talented editor, formatter, marketer, counselor, and cheerleader, and the sister I'm so lucky to call my own—for bringing both clarity and heart to every step of this journey.

Deep gratitude as well to Kathryn Eifert, my sweet daughter, for her thoughtful proofreading and steady encouragement; to my niece, Elise Kraft, for nudging me to weave in the stories that make this guide come alive; and to my brother-in-law, Brian Monkarsh, whose keen eye and profound support gave me renewed confidence.

To my son and his beautiful bride, Austin and Cassidy Eifert, thank you for your love, humor, and support that keep me grounded and grateful.

Warm appreciation to my dear family and friends for their thoughtful contributions: Paul and Teri Hamel, Bob and Leslie Branyon, Beth Graham, Traci Evling, Jane Sullivan, Eva Del Rio, and Mary Beth Buda.

My thanks as well to Gretchen Titshaw, whose courage in sharing her own journey became a quiet spark for me, before I even knew I was looking for one. And to Pam Bergeson, our financial advisor, whose steady expertise and thoughtful coaching have helped us set—and continually reset—a financial plan we trust, bringing clarity and confidence along the way.

To the friends, family members, and clients who trusted me enough to share their stories and transitions: your courage, humor, and honesty shaped this guide more than you know.

And finally, to you, the reader—thank you for stepping into this new season with curiosity, heart, and resilience. I hope this guide becomes a companion you return to whenever you need a reminder that thriving is always within reach.

Author's Note

I didn't set out to write a book.

I set out to make sense of the strange in-between space that opened up after the calendar stopped being filled by work, kids, and deadlines. I was used to purpose showing up in a hurry. But in retirement, it whispers—or sometimes hides altogether.

This guide is the result of years of reflection, conversation, coaching, and lived experience—my own and others'. It's not meant to tell you how to live, but to help you listen more closely to yourself.

Think of it less like a manual and more like a compass. Mark it up. Tab the sections. Skip around. This isn't school—it's your life.

— Beth Eifert

www.ingramcontent.com/pod-product-compliance
Lightning Source LLC
LaVergne TN
LVHW081318110826
845149LV00006B/1538

9798994530511